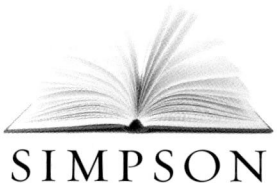

# SIMPSON

IMPRINT IN HUMANITIES

The humanities endowment
by Sharon Hanley Simpson and
Barclay Simpson honors
MURIEL CARTER HANLEY
whose intellect and sensitivity
have enriched the many lives
that she has touched.

*The publisher and the University of California Press Foundation gratefully acknowledge the generous support of the Simpson Imprint in Humanities.*

Passion Relics and the Medieval Imagination

THE FRANKLIN D. MURPHY LECTURE SERIES

*David Cateforis, Series Editor (2014- )*

Established in 1979 through the Kansas University Endowment Association in honor of former chancellor Dr. Franklin D. Murphy, the Murphy Lectureship in Art brings distinguished art historians, critics, and artists to the University of Kansas, where they participate in the teaching of a graduate seminar in the Kress Foundation Department of Art History and deliver two public lectures, one at the Spencer Museum of Art and one at the Nelson-Atkins Museum of Art, the published versions of which are presented in this series.

THE FRANKLIN D. MURPHY LECTURERS IN ART

| Year | Lecturer | Year | Lecturer |
|---|---|---|---|
| 1979 | Pierre Rosenberg | 1996 | Karal Ann Marling |
| 1980 | Brian O'Doherty | 1996 | John M. Rosenfield |
| 1981 | Xia Nai | 1998 | Serafín Moralejo |
| 1982 | Richard Field | 1999 | Helmut Brinker |
| 1983 | Robert G. Calkins | 2001 | Yi Sŏng-mi |
| 1983 | Svetlana Alpers | 2001 | Wanda M. Corn |
| 1984 | Nubuo Tsuji | 2003 | Donald McCallum |
| 1986 | David Rosand | 2004 | Roberta Smith |
| 1987 | James Cahill | 2005 | Tamar Garb |
| 1987 | William Vaughan | 2007 | Okwui Enwezor |
| 1988 | Walter S. Gibson | 2008 | David M. Lubin |
| 1989 | Thomas Lawton | 2009 | Christopher M. S. Johns |
| 1990 | Johei Sasaki | 2010 | Toshio Watanabe |
| 1992 | Marilyn Aronberg Lavin and Irving Lavin | 2012 | Michael Brenson |
| | | 2014 | Cynthia Hahn |
| 1994 | Lothar Ledderose | 2017 | Christine Guth |
| 1994 | John Szarkowski | 2018 | Erika Doss |

# Passion Relics and the Medieval Imagination

*Art, Architecture, and Society*

CYNTHIA HAHN

UNIVERSITY OF CALIFORNIA PRESS

*in association with the Spencer Museum of Art and Kress Foundation Department of Art History, the University of Kansas*

*The publisher gratefully acknowledges the generous contributions to this book provided by the University of Kansas Provost's Office and the Franklin D. Murphy Lecture Fund through the Spencer Museum of Art and the Kress Foundation Department of Art History, the University of Kansas.*

University of California Press
Oakland, California

© 2020 by Cynthia Hahn

Library of Congress Cataloging-in-Publication Data

Names: Hahn, Cynthia J. (Cynthia Jean), author.
Title: Passion relics and the Medieval imagination : art, architecture, and society / Cynthia Hahn.
Other titles: University of Kansas Franklin D. Murphy lecture series.
Description: Oakland, California : University of California Press, [2020] | Series: The Franklin D. Murphy lecture series | Includes bibliographical references and index.
Identifiers: LCCN 2019010297 | ISBN 9780520305267 (cloth : alk. paper)
Subjects: LCSH: Jesus Christ—Relics. | Christian art and symbolism—Medieval, 500–1500.
Classification: LCC BT465 .H34 2020 | DDC 236.96/6—dc23
LC record available at https://lccn.loc.gov/2019010297

Printed in China

28  27  26  25  24  23  22  21  20  19
10  9  8  7  6  5  4  3  2  1

*for Meara Lockwood and Richard Patrick Callan*

CONTENTS

*Preface and Acknowledgments*   ix

Introduction   1

1. The Lure of Passion Relics, the Power of the Cross   7
    *The True Cross*   7
    *Cross—Sign, Image, Thing, Relic*   17
    *The Relic and Its Dispersal—Emperors, Churchmen, and Crusaders*   30
    *Jerusalem Crosses and the Toulouse Châsse*   35

2. Passion Relics: Strength in Unity   51
    *Instruments of Torture*   51
    *Passion Relics as Things*   63
    *Passion Relics Collected*   79
    *Devotion to Passion Relics*   101
    *The* Arma Christi   103
    *Conclusion*   118

*Notes*   121
*Bibliography*   135
*List of Illustrations*   149
*Index*   153
*Biblical Citations*   159

PREFACE AND
ACKNOWLEDGMENTS

This small book began as the Murphy lectures, delivered at the Spencer Museum of Art at the University of Kansas and at the Nelson-Atkins Museum in Kansas City. Receptive audiences encouraged me to think that the subject was one that others would find of interest. It is not, perhaps, an obvious art historical topic—the relics and especially their reliquaries have no visual similarity that identifies them as a group. Some are very beautiful, others are not.

Rather, it is some sense of the relics forming a group, telling a story, and so often being collected as a set that makes this subject a worthwhile topic. As I hope I demonstrate in these essays, they come to take up residence in the medieval imagination as testimony to the Passion as well as a provocation to prayer. How their presentation as relics enlarges the cult and devotion to the suffering Christ is a question at the heart of my endeavor.

The text here, especially the second chapter is extensively revised from the lectures as delivered, for the sake of clarity. As with the museum lectures, I hope my audience includes beginning students, advanced scholars, and curious members of the public, each of whom want to delve into this material. As must be obvious from this statement and from the initial structure—two short lectures—of course, this is the briefest of sketches. It is to be hoped that others who pursue the study will fill in the many gaps and take the material further toward many and unanticipated ends.

For their help in this endeavor, I wish to thank a number of people. Anne D. Hedeman and Sally Cornelison invited me to give the lectures and to teach with them in a seminar titled "Framing the Sacred in Medieval and Early Modern Europe." The Kansas seminar students—Emily Beran, Sean Kramer, Ashley Offill, Sadie Shillieto, and Cristi Slocum—made up the important core of the audience for this material and were a wonderful group of interlocutors.

The Kress Foundation Department of Art History at Kansas is a remarkable and vital program, especially given the possibilities provided by the Franklin D. Murphy endowment and other bequests, including that from medieval scholar and long-time professor in the department Marilyn Stokstad.

I thank the then-chair of the department, Linda Stone-Ferrier; Spencer Museum director Saralyn Reece Hardy; and Nelson-Atkins director Julian Zugazagoitia for their support of my visit, as well as the art history department's office manager Lisa Cloar for all of her organizational help. Graduate student Sara James Dyer has served most recently as an excellent research assistant on the project, acquiring photographs and interfacing with the press. David Cateforis is the amiable editor of the Murphy Lecture Series and present chair of the department. All of these Kansans were invaluable in bringing this project to its conclusion.

Of course, I also owe much gratitude to my husband, John Davies, who has patiently listened, attended lectures, read and critiqued, cooked, and traveled with me. I sincerely doubt I would accomplish anything without him.

In these less formal acknowledgments, John Hedeman also deserves warm thanks for helping to make our short residence in Lawrence so delightful.

I wish, however, to dedicate the book to my daughter, Meara Lockwood, and to the little boy she and her husband brought into the world during this book's gestation. Richard Patrick Callan, named after the grandfather he never met, is already a student of all he sees and a promise of the future.

# Introduction

The True Cross is, without question, the preeminent relic of Christianity. It is the first among a group called the Passion relics—that is, the objects venerated as part of the story of Christ's torment and crucifixion. Alert a group of believers that a fragment of the Cross may be seen, and heads will pivot eagerly, seeking its presence—eyes will be lifted, prayers begun. However, it must be admitted that in the complex environment of worship, devotees can rarely see such a relic with any clarity, and rather than through vision, the impact of the relic is experienced via "presence" and community. Given that many relics of the True Cross are only the tiniest of splinters, by necessity it is the reliquary, the container for those relics, that "makes" the relic present and allows it "visibility." Thus it might be said that, contrary to common sense, devout eyes are focused on the reliquary rather than the relic itself.

The Venetian Renaissance painter Titian captures the effect admirably (fig. 1). His portrait of the male members of the Vendramin family in the presence of the Cross relic of the Scuola Grande di San Giovanni Evangelista (1543–47) shows a variety of responses, from unaware to pious to rapt. The Cross reliquary, gleaming dimly via the rock crystal and gold that frame its precious contents, is elevated on the holy altar and honored by burning candles, but it remains a diminutive object in the upper right corner of the painting. Notably, through the participants' gestures and outward-directed

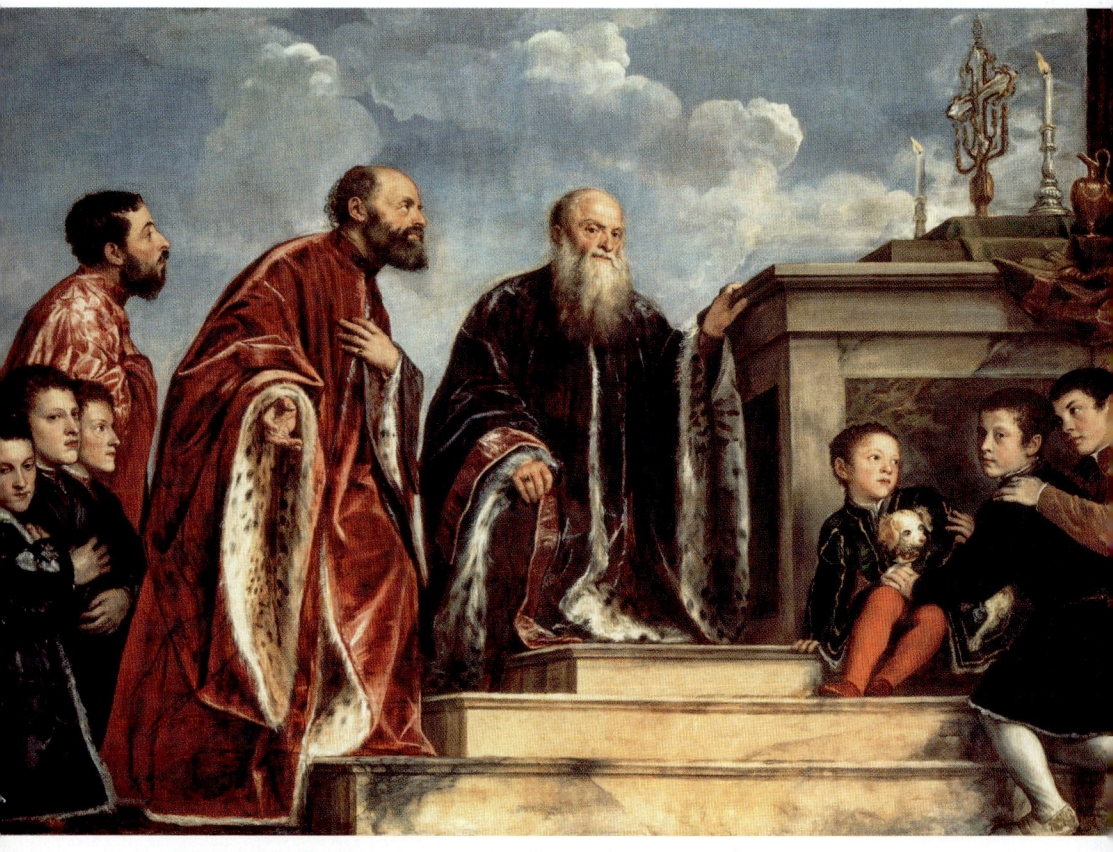

Figure 1. Titian (Tiziano Vecelli), *The Vendramin Family*, painted for Scuola Grande di San Giovanni Evangelista, c. 1547. Oil on canvas, 206 × 301 cm. National Gallery, London. (Photo: © akg-images)

gazes, we, the viewers of the painting, are graciously invited to enter into a social identity that is constituted through devotion to the sacred relic.

This brief description of Titian's painting succinctly introduces us to the issues that complicate our understanding of relics and their presentation via reliquaries. We must begin by attending to materiality, sight, devotion, audience, and community. In the two essays that follow, rather than scrutinize the Passion relics themselves, we focus on the social and cultural phenomena surrounding them. Our concern centers on the presentation and reception of the relics; that is, we examine their reliquaries and display environment, as well as the history of devotions to them. Before launching such an inquiry, however, a few basic questions must be asked—and the answers may seem disconcerting and paradoxical to the reader.

The first question, of course, is, What are relics? Simply put, they are sacred remains, but one must admit that is not a very satisfactory answer. It presupposes that two key questions are already resolved: one concerns the means of selection of the remains, and the other, even more fundamental, a definition of the sacred.

Relics, it must be said, are part of a ubiquitous but misunderstood historical and religious category. All the while that they assert their status as material objects, at the same time they serve a purpose that is distinctly opposite to their physical nature. That is, the primary effect and definition of a relic is a thing that evokes memories and recalls absent persons, places, and events. Relics draw the eye toward what may be abject materiality—dust, bone, splinters, and base matter—engaging the body and the senses, but simultaneously relics deny mundane reality and redirect attention heavenward, toward the divine (as with Titian's subjects). As we will see, reliquaries, art, and architecture are an essential aspect of this most fundamental redirection, this heavenward turn. Art helps us to know where to look, how to look, what to see, and how to react. Thus, the task of definition is already mired in the problematic question of how the material can evoke the immaterial.

The second issue is perhaps more basic. It is commonly assumed today that a relic is some sort of bodily remnant of a saint, perhaps a bone, and thus usually a thing that is revolting to modern viewers. None of the Passion relics, however, are bones. As we pursue our topic, we will find that relics of the Passion appear in an astounding variety of forms and materials but are never bodily relics. So, the second question is, What are Passion relics and how are they selected? The only satisfactory answer is that they are associated with the events of Christ's torment and death rather than having any physical likeness to one another.

Other equally misleading assumptions and questions misdirect our understanding about these relics. A third issue zeroes in on questions of "truth." Viewers persuaded by the rhetoric of staging established by the sacred aura of reliquary and environment assume that what they see is authentic. That is, they accept the relics as real, unique, and powerful because the displays seem to promise that relics are delivered directly to the viewer, without mediation, from a moment of origin in martyrdom or miracle. As such, relics are presented as persistent, even eternal in their testimony as material objects, miraculously so.[1] Further consideration, however, reveals that relics are neither entirely "true" nor entirely "false," and they are often, undeniably, subject to the opposite of timelessness—that is, they are contingent and, as we will see, historically constrained. Sometimes they rot or disappear.

Finally, we might ask, as a subset of the already problematic category of relics, How do Passion relics measure up to expectations? To be sure, they present a very special case and yet another paradox. They are the primary "dominical" relics, those that represent Christ. And, although Christ's *body* is central to the events fundamental to Christian faith—his Incarnation, his Crucifixion, and his Resurrection—that body is entirely unavailable. With the possible exception of blood shed during the Passion,[2] Christ's body with all of its parts, according to Christian doctrine, ascended in its entirety to Heaven.

Given this stunning absence, yet at the same time the need to satisfy the material preoccupations and devotions of Christianity, alternative objects appear. What might in other circumstances be classified as lesser, or "contact," relics—that is, instruments of torture that touched Christ's body during his Passion—become the principal focus of Christian prayer. However, questions of identification and of course provenance, leave us at something of a loss. Unlike the bodily relics of the saints, very few legends detailing the origin and preservation of Passion relic-objects survive. Instead, as we will see, most strikingly in the case of the Crown of Thorns, various objects mysteriously and spontaneously surface and are celebrated.

Indeed, it can be argued that rather than being persistent or eternal, Passion relics seem to emerge, in their sudden appearances, in response to specific Christian devotional needs. That is, as questions about the nature of Christ and his worship arose or developed during the Middle Ages and later, relics as manifestations of material Christianity "made themselves known" in order to reassure and support the congregations of the faithful, to aid in their prayers, or perhaps in some cases, more venally, to serve political purposes. Ultimately, it is not our concern to question the authenticity of these objects (surely some were manufactured—whether for unprincipled or devotional motives we cannot say), but such manifestations allow us to consider Passion relics not only as holy material but also as social phenomena—as barometers of Christian devotion and its processes.

So, in contrast to the commonsense perception of relics discussed above—that each is eternal, singular, and intrinsically sacred—in this study we will consider a different scenario: that relics are objects that have histories and multiplicities, that they are objects that appear and even disappear. In sum, the primary concern of these essays is to briefly tell the story, or stories, of the Passion relics. I hope thus to depict the relics more clearly, to pierce the veil of the fixed religious presentation of such objects of veneration, and to reopen a discussion of their preeminent place as actors in medieval history and art history.

Notably, relics were employed in remarkably varied uses and served a wide range of audiences. Among an infinite number of possible themes and histories, those discussed in these essays include: the early imperial use of

Passion relics as trophies of victory; the development of relics, especially the True Cross as a dual "thing," both sign and potent material object; the persistent medieval engagement with the relics in the context of pilgrimage; the acquisition, multiplication, and spread of the relics during the Crusades; the use of the Passion and Holy Land relics to effect an importation of the sacred from the Jerusalem to other places; and the devotional use of Passion relics (and their images in such depictions as the *Arma Christi*) in imaginative exercises of prayer. Although this list follows a roughly chronological development, the material that follows is not organized in strictly chronological fashion but ventures to offer a brief thematic overview of some of the major relics—cross, nails, lance, crown of thorns, and a few others—as well as specific examples of their presentation and their collection, in the great European treasuries of the Middle Ages and the Early Modern period.

CHAPTER ONE

# The Lure of Passion Relics, the Power of the Cross

## THE TRUE CROSS

Despite their somewhat mysterious and fraught histories, the relics of Christ's Passion came to be the greatest and most coveted treasures of the Middle Ages. From a very early moment they were venerated and collected, but also widely disseminated. These responses were evident from the beginning in the earliest reception of the greatest of the Passion relics—that of the True Cross.

The deprecatory joke concerning the dissemination of the True Cross in John Calvin's *Treatise on Relics* of 1543—"if we were to collect all these pieces of the True Cross exhibited in various parts, they would form a whole ship's cargo"[1]—finds its origin as early as the fourth century in a markedly more positive assessment. Cyril, bishop of Jerusalem (313–86), boasted that the wood of the Cross "has from here already filled almost the whole world."[2] It was a source of pride to the bishop that myriad splinters had been spread far and wide because such purposeful relic dispersal (largely through gifts) was effective in establishing the influence and power not only of the Cross but also of the Holy City of Jerusalem.

The relic of the Cross (hereafter also called the True Cross to distinguish it from the symbol or image of a cross) had been purportedly discovered on Golgotha by the emperor Constantine's mother, Helena, during an imperial visit to the Holy Land in 326, in the course of which she visited the sites of Christ's life on earth. The trip was only later characterized as a pilgrimage (see figs. 2 and 3).[3] Modern readers may doubt the veracity of the account whereby the empress induced a Jew who purportedly had a family history associated with the Cross to reveal its whereabouts some three centuries and more after the events of the Crucifixion, but surely most Christians accepted the story as truth. Legends further claim that the empress was able to verify the identity of the True Cross among the three she recovered (the others were the crosses of the thieves) by using it to provoke the miracle of the resurrection of a dead man. She subsequently enclosed the relics in silver, gold, and gems, deposited portions of the newly validated relic in Jerusalem, and sent other portions to Rome and Constantinople.

Many stories tell of the further dissemination of the True Cross, but history confirms that the major portion of the relic remained in Jerusalem until it was captured by the Persians in 614 and then recaptured by the Byzantine emperor Heraclius in 629. At that point, the largest portion of the relic was taken to Constantinople.

From the earliest moment of its discovery and therefore throughout its history, the True Cross was associated with the Roman (then Byzantine) empire and its power. Through Helena's actions and gifts and even before, in Constantine's vision of the symbol of the Chi-Rho inscribed with the promise "in hoc signo vinces" (in this sign you will conquer),[4] the cross became a sign of divine support for imperial power, a status that was maintained and even augmented throughout the Middle Ages (see left panel of fig. 2 for an image of Constantine's vision).[5]

In addition to the imperial use and display of the relics, however, the dissemination of fragments of the True Cross by Church leaders such as Cyril and Jerome allowed the cross to serve another equally significant but very different role. The dispersal of the True Cross conformed to—even, in uniquely material fashion, *demonstrated*—the Christian doctrine of the

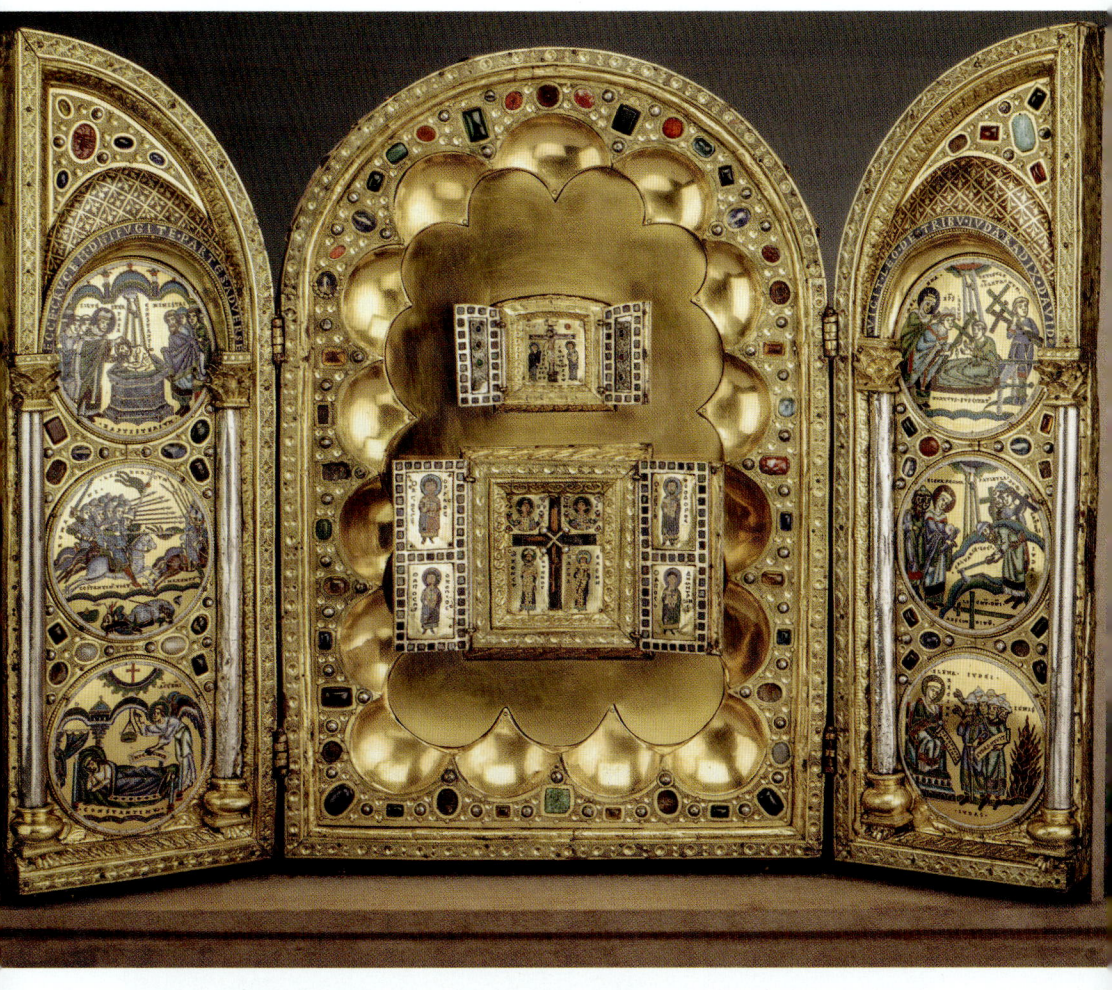

Figure 2. *Stavelot Triptych*, c. 1156–1158. Wood with copper-gilt frames, silver pearls and columns, gilt-brass capitals and bases, vernis brun domes, semiprecious stones, intaglio gems, beads, champlevé and cloisonné enamels, 48.4 × 66 cm. Morgan Library and Museum, New York. (Photo: © Morgan Library and Museum / Art Resource)

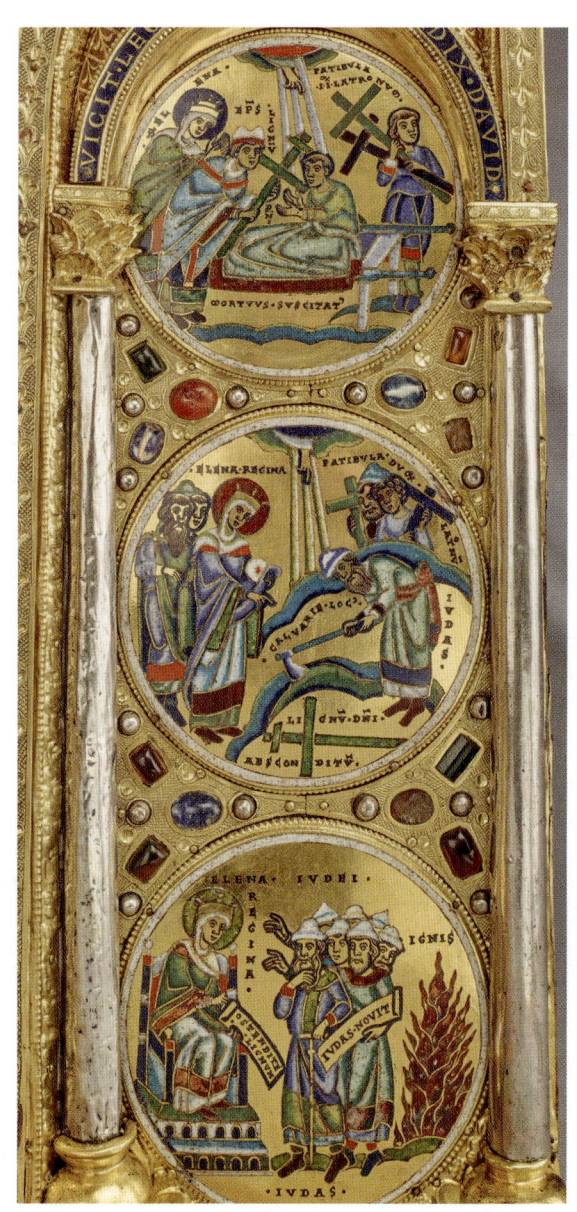

Figure 3. *Stavelot Triptych* (detail), c. 1156–1158. Morgan Library and Museum, New York. (Photo: © Morgan Library and Museum / Art Resource)

universal accessibility of grace. This is the sort of task at which relics excel because of their special ability to mix the material and the spiritual. To understand this spiritual work of relics and reliquaries, particularly that of the True Cross, a brief consideration of the spiritual and theological understanding of the cross will be useful here.

In Judaism, access to reconciliation with God had a very specific but renewable location, one that was constructed by men according to divine specifications delivered to Moses at Sinai. That is, the space between the wings of the cherubim, the "mercy seat" or top of the Ark of the Covenant as placed in the Tabernacle (or Temple), was called the place of propitiation or forgiveness (Exod. 25:17). In that space, particular holy men could encounter the divine and intercede for the Jewish people. In contrast, Christ's sacrifice on the cross allowed Christians access to God's grace and forever superseded the need for the Ark. At the Carolingian oratory of Germigny-des-Prés, an empty ark with cherubim is depicted in the apse mosaic of the church. Surely a cross stood on the altar in front of this mosaic. (fig.4).

The Ark of the Covenant is in some sense the prototype for all Christian reliquaries, including reliquaries of the Cross. The creation of powerful spaces comparable to the Ark and Temple, where material welcomes immaterial and where the earthly could receive the heavenly, was ultimately the goal of medieval reliquaries. Moreover, I will argue that any cross—an object that can be symbol, relic, *and* reliquary—in itself creates a powerful and divine space through its inherent theatricality, physicality, and aura. Indeed, as one of the most potent and active of all medieval signs or objects, in Christian terms, the cross in its invocation of sacrifice is understood to replace the Ark. Alternately, one can think of the Ark as welcoming the Cross as at Germigny. Christ's death becomes the last blood sacrifice in the place of propitiation.

A more explicit visualization of this elision of Ark and True Cross can be seen in the iconography of the "Throne of Mercy." In discussing this image,

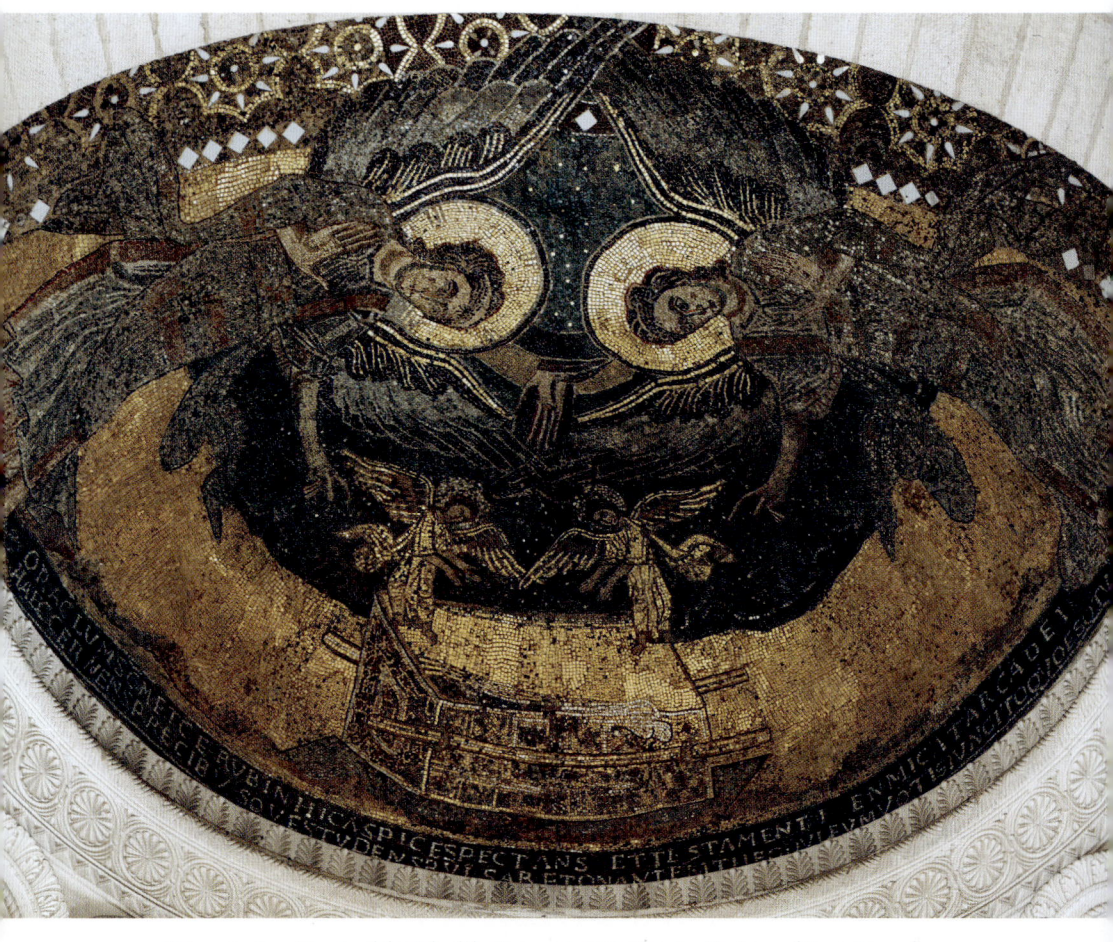

Figure 4. *Apse Mosaic of the Ark of the Covenant*, 806. Mosaic. Oratory of Germigny-des-Prés, Dép. Loiret, France. (Photo: © Leemage / Universal Images Group / Getty Images)

art historians usually focus on the Trinity—that is, the depiction of God the Father holding Christ on the Cross and the two joined by the Holy Spirit. An early stained glass composition from Saint-Denis, commissioned by the renowned Abbot Suger in about 1144, shows, however, that the Ark is an important part of the imagery (fig. 5). In a version of Ezekiel's vision with its wheels, winged beasts, and sapphire throne (Ezek. 1:1–26), the crucified Christ, attached to an emphatically living cross (depicted as green and growing), rises from the space above the central Ark. Although the third person of the Trinity, the Holy Spirit represented by the dove, is missing because of restoration of the glass, the image is a striking representation of divine presence and its power. The inscriptions on the glass note, "On the Ark of the Covenant is established the altar with the Cross of Christ," calling the effect of the Cross "a greater covenant" in reference to the text of Paul's letter to the Hebrews. In that letter Paul further specifies: "But Christ, being come an high priest of good things to come, by a greater and more perfect tabernacle, not made with hands, that is to say, not of this building; neither by the blood of goats and calves, but by his own blood he entered in once into the holy place, having obtained eternal redemption for us" (Heb. 9:11–12).[6] Paul also characterizes the Ark as container "overlaid round about with gold, wherein was the golden pot that had manna, and Aaron's rod that budded, and the tables of the covenant" (Heb. 9:4). If the Ark held the tablets of the Law, the rod of Aaron, and the pot of manna, in a sense it was a reliquary space dedicated to the Jewish religion. In turn it was claimed by the Cross and Christianity and became the heavenly throne of the vision of Ezekiel. In the depiction of the stained glass, God looks out, holding the cross and in forgiveness invites the viewer into this space.

Although in the Saint-Denis glass, the cross is only one part of a complex symbol of divine power, the image clearly summons the authority of the True Cross relic. The green and living wood emphasizes the materiality of the relic and its derivation from a living, earthly substance.[7] Furthermore,

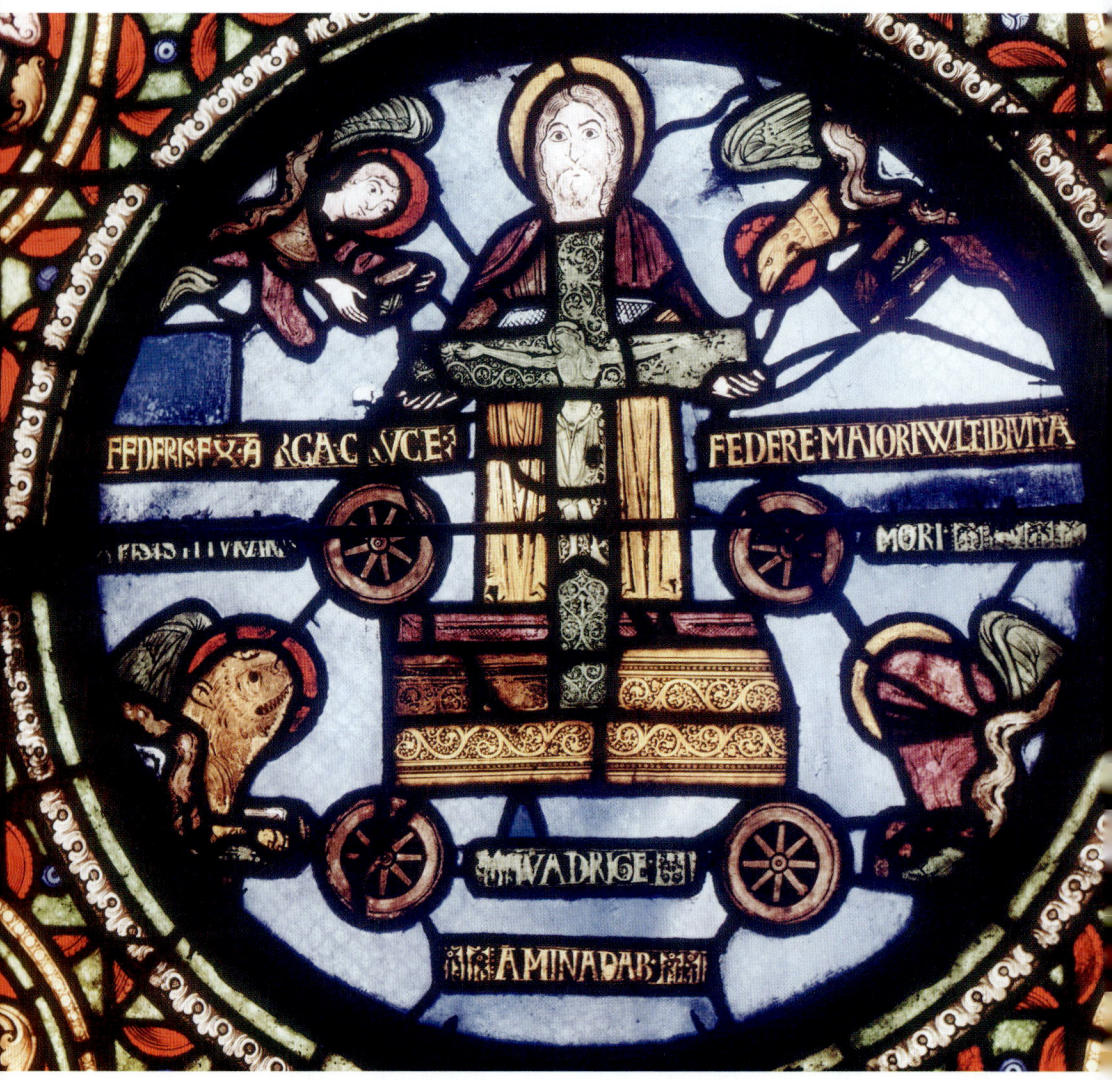

Figure 5. *"Quadriga of Aminadab"* (detail from Allegories of Saint Paul window), 12th century. Stained glass. Abbey Church, Saint-Denis, France. (Photo: © RMN–Grand Palais / Art Resource)

the foot of the cross arises from the Ark, where the other "testimonies" or relics were stored. In other words, the cross takes its place among the Old Testament relics, all the while superseding them.

Many medieval reliquaries, especially True Cross reliquaries, recall this scenario of the material cross taking a focal position. For example, in the twelfth-century the *Triptych Reliquary of the Cross*, now in the Wyvern Collection (fig. 6), we might see the paired angels on the central panel as recalling the cherubim of the Ark, although they also represent honor guards of the "sign of the Son of Man" (Matt. 24:30), the Cross returned at the end of days for the Last Judgment.[8] With a gentle demonstrative touch, the angels present a rectangular cavity, once enclosed with rock crystal and sheltering a relic of the True Cross but now missing its relic and covered with replacement glass. The cavity, in its shape, is reminiscent of the rectangular surface of the "mercy seat" or place of atonement. On the wings of the triptych, angels blow the trumpets to call the dead from their graves, and below the relic at center, Justicia weighs the scales, judging *omnes gentes* (all the people), with Misericordia and Pietas (Mercy and Piety). On a small pediment above, Christ in heaven opens his arms, displaying his wounds and gesturing to the Crown of Thorns on his right and the bowl of vinegar (often associated with the devil) on his left, representing both the Judge and the alternatives of his Judgment: the blessed crown or damning bitterness.[9] In such Christian visions of the Ark/reliquary, the viewer is invited into the space and the angels serve as participants—that is, rather than defending the space, facing one another and covering it with their wings as in Exodus 26:20, the cherubim welcome viewers into the holy space (as also at Germigny, fig. 4). The inclusion of the figures of Prayer (Oratio) and Alms-giving (Elemosyna) as well as the Instruments of the Passion is further evidence that the Wyvern triptych Judgment imagery, rather than being a threat of damnation, served as a call to penitence and good works and a promise of the life-saving qualities of the True Cross and Passion relics.[10]

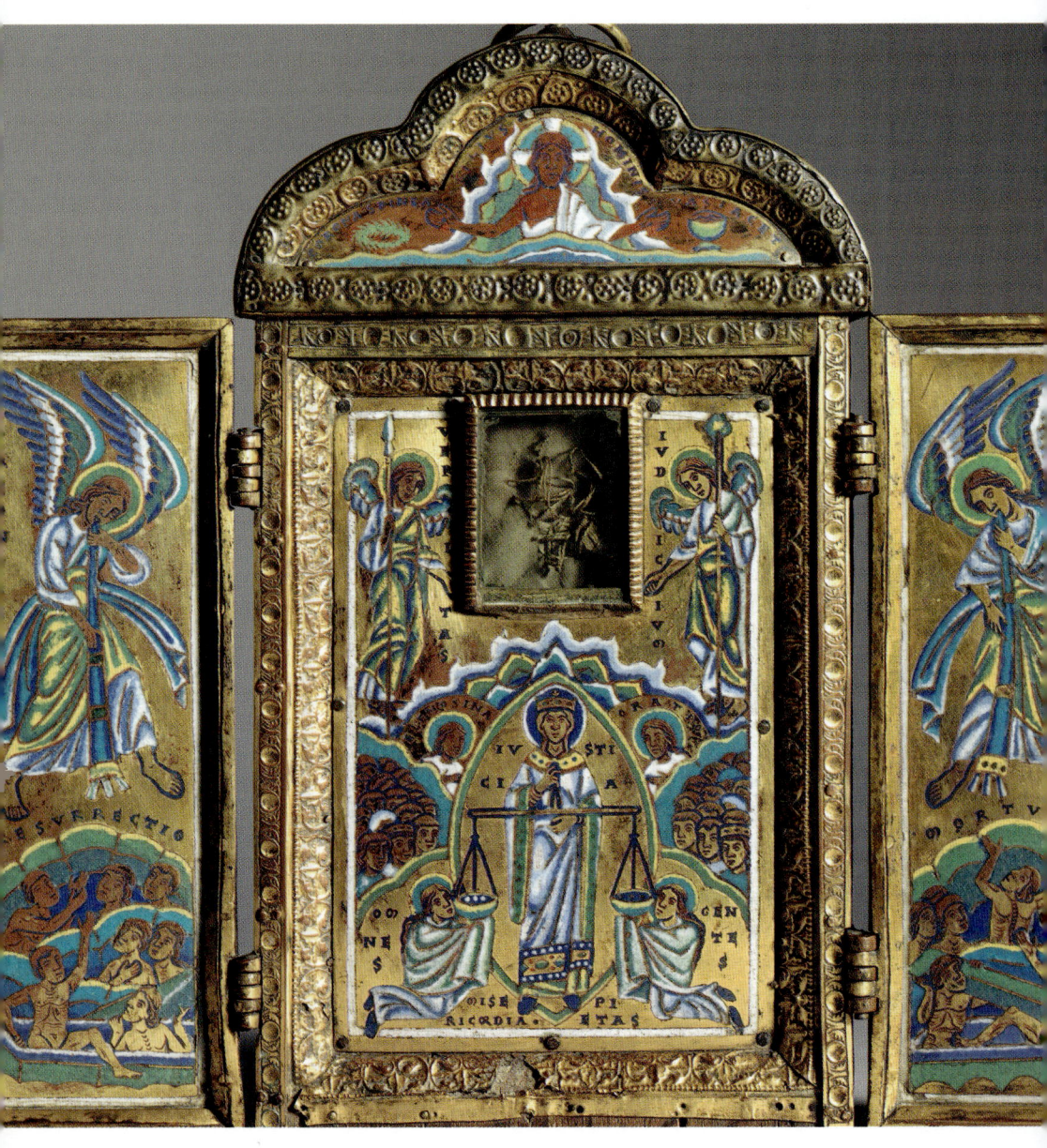

In short, in our brief exploration of these various topics (the dissemination of relics, the conceptual origins of reliquaries, and the purpose and place of the Cross in salvation history as shown in art), we have already begun to intimate the preeminent importance of the Cross and its relics and the potential complexity of its interactions with believers. Let us however, as proposed a moment ago, delve deeper into the meaning of the Cross as a verbal and visual sign and further explore its use in liturgy and its history as a relic, especially in its earliest Christian appearances.

### CROSS—SIGN, IMAGE, THING, RELIC

The Biblical meaning of the cross lies in its nonverbal yet signative nature. In 1 Corinthians (1:17-18) Paul preaches "not with wisdom of words" but with the cross, "for the preaching of the cross is to them that perish foolishness; but unto us which are saved it is the power of God." In a tenth-century manuscript from Reichenau with scenes of the life of the martyr Romanus (fig. 7), the saint preaches in this manner. The text recounts the saint's testimony to pagan prosecutors about the powers of the cross, but never mentions a physical cross. Nonetheless, as Romanus despairs that he is "casting pearls before swine,"[11] he holds a golden cross as demonstrative protection and witness. Here the cross is both Christian truth and physical *thing*.[12]

In a similar combination of idea and object, Eusebius, the biographer of the first Christian emperor, casts Constantine's dream vision of the cross as simultaneously a moment of conversion and a divine order to make a material cross, "to make a likeness of that sign which he had seen in the heavens, and to use it as a safeguard in all engagements with his enemies." Of course it was also that same momentous dream that promised the emperor victory

Figure 6. *Triptych Reliquary of the Cross*, c. 1160-70. Gilded copper, champlevé enamel, émail brun, and rock crystal, 27 × 29.2 cm. Wyvern Collection, United Kingdom. (Photo: © Wyvern Collection)

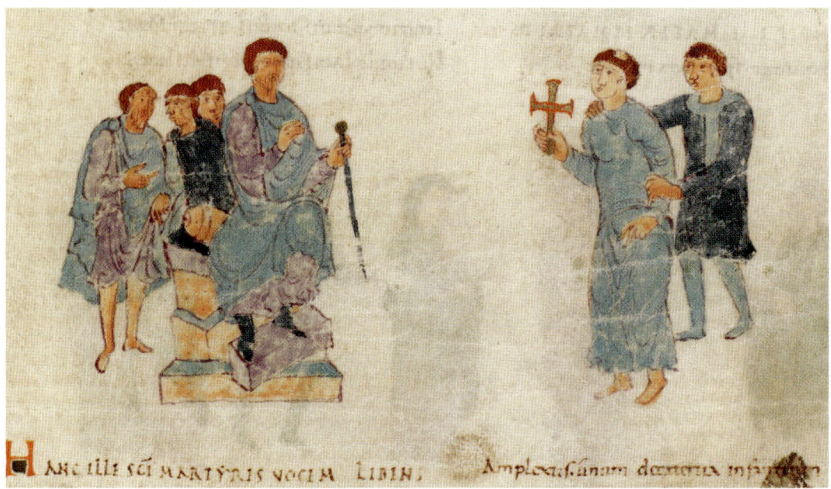

Figure 7. "Scenes of the Life of the Martyr Romanus," in Prudentius, *Carmina*, Cod. 264, p. 135, c. 900. Parchment manuscript, 27.3/28.3 × 21.5/22 cm. Burgerbibliothek, Bern. (Photo: Burgerbibliothek, Bern; e-codices: www.e-codices.unifr.ch/en/list/one/bbb/0264)

through Christ's sign and initiated the notion of the cross as a trophy, the "sign of salvation as a safeguard against every adverse and hostile power."[13] Even though all this occurred *before* the True Cross was discovered and identified by Constantine's mother, the empress Helena, the dream revelation and discovery of the Cross were quickly brought together in legend (see figs. 2 and 3).

Just as a cross can materialize from potent words, convert its viewers, or prevail as a formidable battle standard, its presence as an object can consistently and powerfully impress Christians as well as spur action and emotional response. In its rich evocation of associations, the cross is a remarkable example of semiosis—that is, as semiotic theory would understand it, the unstoppable fluidity and flow of meaning. It is therefore no surprise that, to its unparalleled status as thing and not-thing, as lump of heavy wood yet

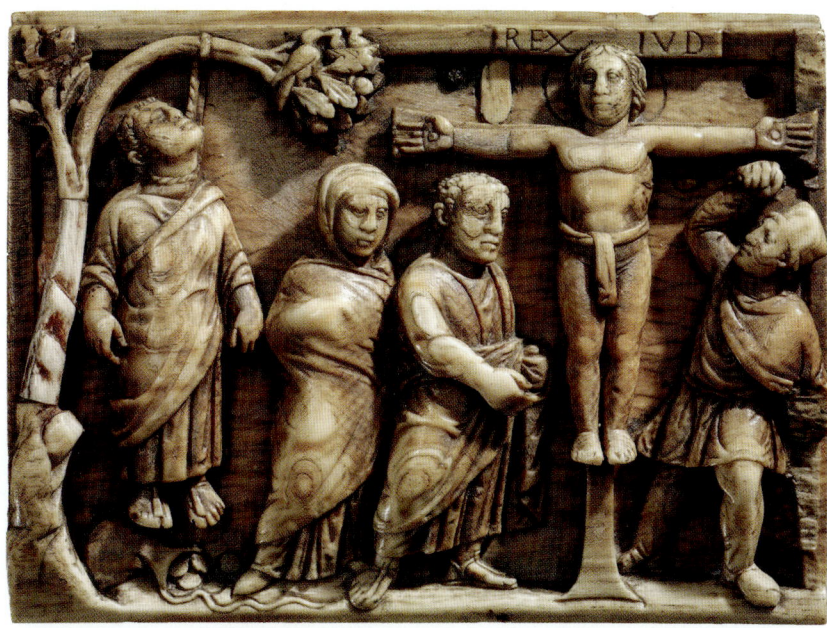

Figure 8. *The Death of Judas and the Crucifixion*, c. 420–430 CE. Ivory casket plaque, 7.5 × 10.2 cm. British Museum, London. (Photo: © Trustees of the British Museum. All rights reserved.)

also sign, another meaning should be added: that of the multivalent and powerful idea of the cross as relic

Strikingly, one of the very earliest images of the Crucifixion already exhibited two distinctly different manifestations of the cross. The early fifth-century ivory plaque in the British Museum (part of a box that was most likely a reliquary) depicts Christ suspended on what appears to be the likeness of a metal processional or ceremonial cross with distinctively flared ends (fig. 8).[14] It would seem that, in this early representation, in order to make sense of the cross, the narrative of the Passion is presented as if already embedded in prayer and liturgy. In this way the depiction of the upright

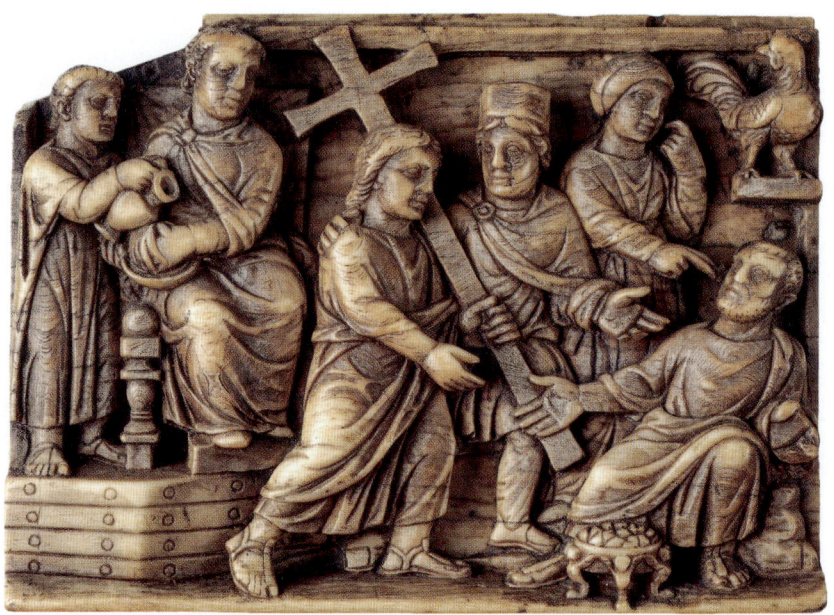

Figure 9. *Pilate and Christ Carrying the Cross*, c. 420–430 CE. Ivory casket plaque, 7.5 × 9.8 cm. British Museum, London. (Photo: © Trustees of the British Museum. All rights reserved.)

figure of Christ with open eyes is made to speak to the Christian concept of victory over death. In a second image, on another plaque from this same little ivory box, Christ is carrying the cross, which has lost the flared ends and is small enough that Christ's hand wraps entirely around it, holding it in a rather intimate and possessive manner, carrying the very long-stemmed object as if, in fact, in procession (fig. 9).

In this pictorial transformation of the wooden instrument of death into a portable object made of metal, and from a massive, heavy (perhaps threatening) cross into one that seems precious and personal, we see the two of the natures of the cross powerfully asserted. The cross is both the means of torture and death, but also at the same time the cross of victory and salvation through prayer. This paradoxical duality will persist as a quality of the cross throughout its history in art and thought, and it also, as we will see, will emerge as an essential characteristic of all Passion relics.

Processions were important opportunities for visual manifestations of crosses, moments when they could be seen by devotees. However, many processional and/or reliquary crosses are smaller than one would expect for objects of public display to large crowds. In the Venetian painting by Gentile Bellini (1496), another from the series in the Scuola Grande di San Giovanni Evangelista (fig. 10; cf. fig. 1), it is difficult to locate the reliquary or the attendant miracle. In the Bellini painting, the cross is just below the processional canopy in the center of the image, and the man dressed in red, falling to his knees to the right attests to the miracle. The small size of the cross in such instances may be due to the fact that crosses, even reliquary crosses, were always intended to be held and moved, either by devotee or celebrant.

I want to emphasize that crosses are complex and demanding but also accommodating. Bodies and crosses interact in a number of ways, and as Sible de Blaauw argues, crosses should not usually be categorized as one type or another—processional crosses or altar crosses; they are generally multifunctional.[15] I will argue that such multifunctionality again realizes them as a sort of super-thing—fully material but also fully entwined with minds, bodies, and emotions. A cross need not even be a reliquary to carry these many meanings. As a Carolingian liturgical commentator noted: "Still the virtue of the Holy True Cross [a relic cross] is not wanting in those crosses which are made in imitation of it."[16]

In writing about Eastern, or Orthodox, practice, Glenn Peers emphasizes the relation of the cross and the body. He argues that in the sixth and seventh centuries the "cross shaped crucifix" (that is, an art object with a representation of Christ) was "a significantly new class of object" that "posits the assimilation of Christian bodies, the body of Christ, and the individual

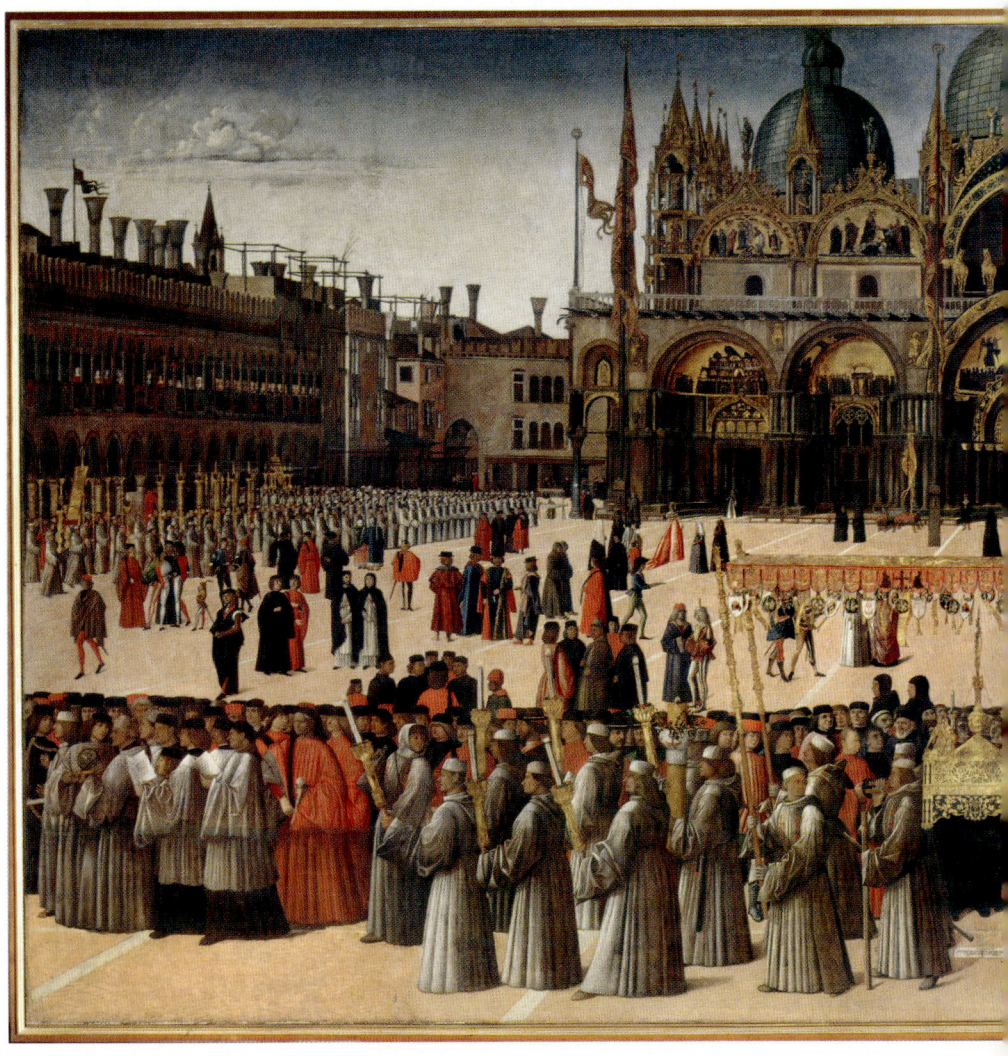

Figure 10. Gentile Bellini, *Procession of the True Cross*, painted for Scuola Grande di San Giovanni Evangelista, 1496. Oil on canvas, 367 × 745 cm. Gallerie dell'Accademia, Venice. (Photo: © akg-images / Cameraphoto)

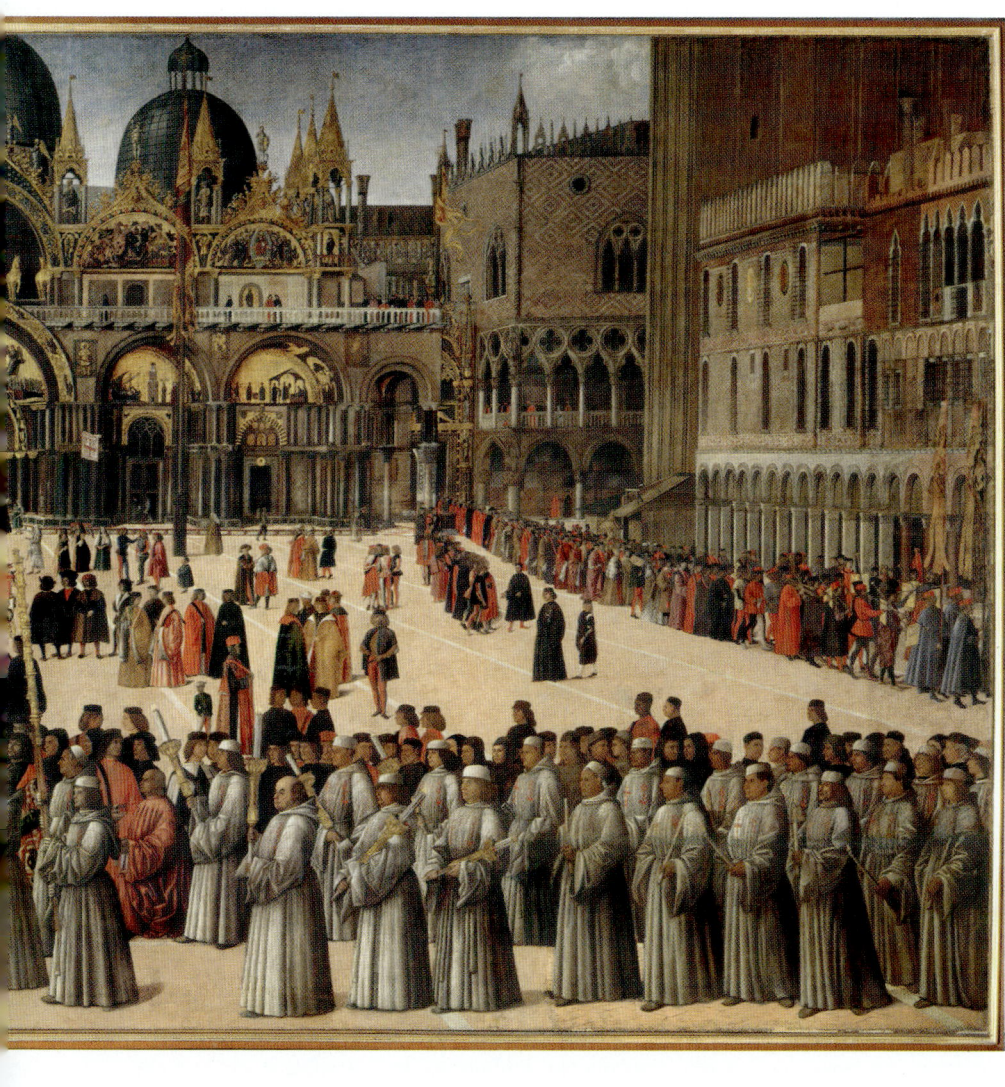

Christian."[17] A seventh-century text concerning monastic devotion to the cross describes the actions of a monk that realize that assimilation:

> Although the man of our Lord Christ in the flesh sits in heaven on the throne of majesty, . . . yet His power, His glory, His working and His dominion are in the cross and you kiss our Lord Himself and embrace Him with love, . . . until your heart is stirred and burns in His love. . . . Stand therefore, . . . with alertness and zest; make the sign of the Cross on your mouth with the crucifix. . . . If you practice these exertions and do not yield to dejectedness, your mind will be uplifted.[18]

This early text speaks to an intersection of a number of realities—the object of a cross, its connection to God in heaven, and the capability of the vision of the cross when combined with prayer to lift the mind. Similar sorts of reactions to the cross can be found throughout Christian devotional history. Bodies conform to the cross, or in the case of Saint Francis and the stigmata, are marked by it. Even if Peers is discussing a simple cross, many personal reliquary crosses survive from the Eastern world in this period and are especially common as pilgrimage objects from the tenth century onward (fig. 11).

Although there were also personal crosses, reliquaries, and phylacteries used in this way in Europe, we should look to the liturgical celebration of the cross in congregational settings as the primary locus of the development of devotion to the cross. In addition to processions that required crosses, the rapid spread of the foremost liturgical feast, the Exaltation of the Cross, celebrated on September 14, attests to the importance of material crosses in early medieval Christian ritual from as early as the fourth century in Jerusalem.[19] The feast appeared in Rome by the seventh century and in the Frankish lands by the eighth.[20]

The feast specifically amplifies and deepens the association of the cross form with the True Cross relic. Just as relic doctrine maintains that relics are not merely earthly remnants but connect the once living body of a saint to his

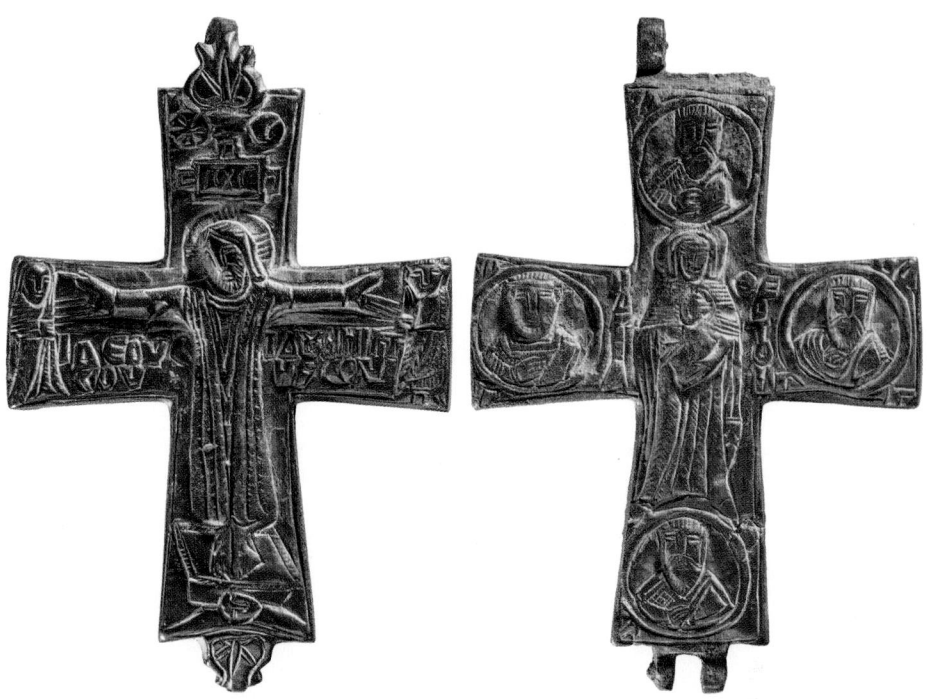

Figure 11. *Pectoral Reliquary Cross*, 9th–10th century. Bronze, front leaf: 12.5 × 7.9 × 1 cm, back leaf: 12.2 × 7.9 × 1 cm. British Museum, London (1985,0305.1). (Photo: © Trustees of the British Museum. All rights reserved.)

or her presence in the heavenly court, the early medieval liturgy of the *Exaltation of the Cross* manifests the dual nature of the cross, binding a physical cross with a glorious vision of a gemmed cross in heaven: "the blessed cross glitters [*nitet*], on which the Lord hung in his flesh, and with his blood washed away our sins."[21] The physical nature of the cross is also emphasized—the True Cross is even described as having a smell: "When the Cross was brought back from out of the land of the Persians, its pleasant odor permeated the Lord's Jerusalem. . . . Through this the noses and hearts of all were refreshed."[22]

Just as the Eastern monk discussed above carried these lessons into his personal devotions, similar practices flourished in the West. Nowhere is the complexity of the cross and its meanings better articulated than in the seventh-century Anglo-Saxon poem "The Dream of the Rood."[23] The poem closely parallels an encounter with the cross—perhaps best described as devotional "looking" at a cross or cross reliquary—and demonstrates how signs combined with imaginative prayer and story can further an understanding of the cross, which the poet calls the "urgent beacon" (l. 21).

Most significantly, the "Dream" shows the intrinsic importance of vision to devotion and understanding. The dreamer recalls that "the holy spirits beheld" the cross (l. 11) as did "men over the earth and all this glorious creation" (l. 12). The poet calls his experience "the best of visions" (l. 1), and once again, the cross appearing before his eyes is an exquisite mystical vision. Surely not typical, such a vision represents performed devotions that, in principle, could be experienced through prolonged meditation by any Christian: "Yet as I lay there a long while I beheld sorrowful the tree of the Saviour" (ll. 24–25).

The dreamer speaks at the outset but soon the cross itself begins to speak, to tell its story.[24] The cross is both living "wonderful tree" (l. 4) and yet also "beacon" (l.6), and it is covered both with gems and gold and with blood (ll. 7-9, 16-20). "Through" the gold, the dreamer is "able to perceive" blood (l. 18). He continues, repeating:

> I was frightened by the beautiful vision; I saw that urgent beacon change its covering and colors; sometimes it was soaked with wetness, stained with the coursing of blood, sometimes adorned with treasure. (ll. 21–23)

The emphatic repetition of the dreamer's dual perception calls our attention to the fluid changeability of the cross. We are vividly confronted with an experience of shifting perception, even both at once, an irreconcilable perversion: the sign of glory dripping with gore, that as an "urgent beacon" demands our attention. Our empathy is provoked by this dilemma. What two elements could be more compelling and yet more different? Oozing warm, absorptive blood confronts the glitter and polish of gold and gems.

Despite these oppositions, the poem forges a path of understanding and comprehension and, after the cross itself recounts its history, it claims to reveal "the true way of life" (l. 89) and commands the dreamer to spread the word. Fear is calmed:

> Then there will be no need for any of those to be very afraid
> who bear before them in the breast the best of trees.
> But by means of the rood each soul
> who thinks to dwell with the Ruler
> must seek the kingdom from the earthly way. (ll. 117–21)

So, at last the cross comes to reside in the body of the believer.

Sight is the motivation of this process: "The Dreamer first sees the vision of a glorious cross, wrapped in light, but a cross he cannot truly 'see' until he perceives the implications of the Crucifixion."[25] Rock crystal was used in the cross in figure 12 for its reflective and refractive qualities. Sight is both the starting point and desired end for the process, as well as an embodiment of the pure joy of the act of devotion: "angels gazing in eternity."

Medieval crosses and reliquaries fully embody these ideas of the cross as all-encompassing and compelling. The four "arms" performatively assert the number four, according to patristic commentary of the early Church, recalling the four winds, the four evangelists or their symbolic beasts, the four letters of Adam's name, the four letters of the *titulus* INRI, and the four times that the sinner is called back by the Church.[26] Furthermore, the vine scroll that occurs on many crosses (see fig. 5) would have evoked the life-giving quality of the cross. The materials of many crosses—gems and gold—were, of course, fitting for such an important object: Alcuin called Christ "a most lucid gem more precious than the whole world" with a body "shining

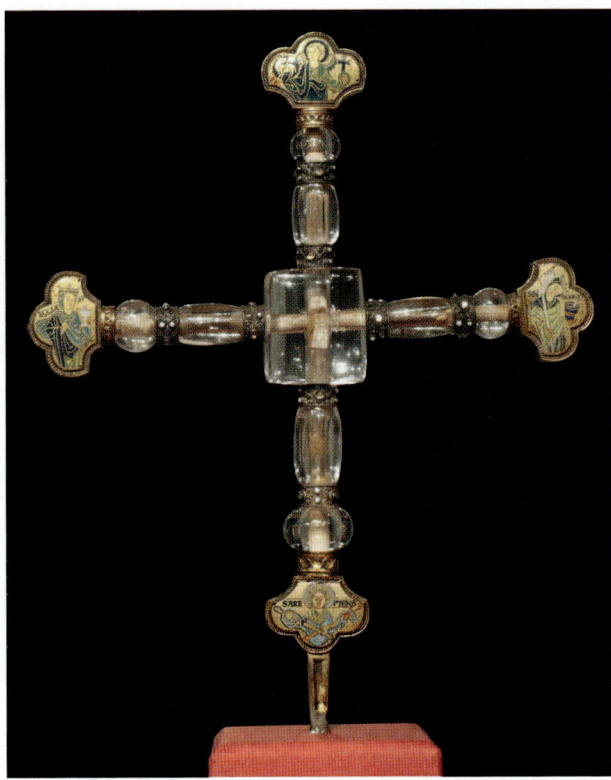

Figure 12. *Scheldewindeke Cross*, c. 1170–1200. Rock crystal, silver, and enamel, 42 × 38.5 cm. Church of St. Christopher, Scheldewindeke, Belgium. (Photo: © Genevra Kornbluth)

like gold tested by fire."[27] Not only were such materials appropriate in order to honor Christ in his relic, but they were also fitting for the often "kingly" or imperial nature of the reliquary commission.[28]

It can even be said that Augustine likened the shape of the cross to the "topology of the moral and spiritual order"; for example, "charity comes from the secret recesses . . . of God's will . . . and this is its depth"[29] Furthermore, Augustine used images from the Passion narrative: Christ's head touched the upright, so it represents hope; the cross's lower end was buried in the earth, so it represents secret depth. Such visual and specific details would have resonated for viewers in their devotions.

Finally, just as in the prayers cited above, devotees were spiritually stamped with the form of the cross. In the act of prayer, they might conform their entire body to the cross shape by raising their arms. In this way, their outstretched hands might mimic Christ's "double charity," and their legs the "columns of Christ's body, that is, the pastors of the church."[30] But of course, primarily, they were sealed by the cross in baptism (with the application of chrism) and would take up the sign of the cross to imitate the suffering of Christ, which could also be captured through the position of prostration and prolonged prayer. In such physical identification with the cross and Christ's suffering, they would begin to feel a profound empathy for and comfort in the cross. In sum, although many cross reliquaries seem remarkably simple in shape and presentation, they have the potential to stimulate a wide variety of devotional meditations, ranging from the contemplation of the meaning of the sign to a focus on the parts and to the evocation of a profound empathy based on positioning and movements of the body.

These are properties shared by most or even all crosses. When we turn, however, from the cross as sign or the cross as used in prayer and liturgy to the third major topic of our investigation, the history of the relic or relics of the Cross, we must deal with the specific rather than the universal. Even if Cyril rejoiced in a unified army of fragments fanning out across the world, spreading the meaning of Christ's sacrifice, it is unavoidably true that among reliquary crosses, there are hierarchies of value and issues of prestige, having to do with size and provenance of relics and circumstances of acquisition and presentation. In other words, some True Cross relics are deemed more important than others.

## THE RELIC AND ITS DISPERSAL—EMPERORS, CHURCHMEN, AND CRUSADERS

Most of the True Cross must have at first remained in Jerusalem, despite Cyril's efforts to disseminate it to influential and important persons who would spread it far and wide:[31] "The holy wood of the Cross gives witness: it is here to be seen this very day, and through those who take [pieces] from it in faith, it has from here already filled almost the whole world."[32] Cyril emphasizes that although the Cross was divided, it was not diminished. Cyril's contemporary, Paulinus, bishop of Nola writes:

> Indeed this Cross of inanimate wood has living power, and ever since its discovery it has lent its wood to the countless, almost daily, prayers of men. Yet it suffers no diminution; though daily divided, it seems to remain whole to those who lift it, and always entire to those who venerate it. Assuredly it draws this power of incorruptibility, this undiminishing integrity, from the Blood of that Flesh which endured death yet did not see corruption.[33]

Of course, Paulinus's assertion corresponds to the more general theology of relics in which a part stands for a larger and complete whole, but it is also a special and even miraculous quality of the Cross that it remains incorruptible and integral on account of the blood that soaked it.

What we also see in Cyril's comments, however, is his attempt to establish provenance for the powerful relics of the Cross, emphasizing that "it is here to be seen this very day," as if it is whole even if also fragmented. This notion of the presence of the relics of the True Cross in the city brings prestige to Jerusalem in the early Christian era.

Meanwhile in Constantinople, Constantine is said to have used at least some portion of the True Cross and its associated relics given him by Helena for various purposes, such as dedicating the new city of Constantinople with the erection of a famous column, topped with a golden statue of himself and founded on a cache of relics.[34] Helena is also said to have deposited a portion of the relic in Rome.[35]

In later historical developments, the Jerusalem relic of the True Cross was captured by the Persians, recovered by Emperor Heraclius in 629, and eventually deposited in Constantinople for safety. In his essay "Eastern Objects and Western Desires," Holger Klein explores how this movement of the major part of the prestigious relic consolidated political power. The True Cross became the cherished possession of the Byzantine emperors as leaders of the Eastern Church. In turn, it became the most coveted of imperial gifts, as well as an instrument of diplomacy and obligation in relationships between the Eastern and Western medieval rulers.[36]

Significant gifts of the relic were made by Byzantine emperors to both ecclesiastical and royal recipients. Those who received splinters include Roman popes and the Frankish Queen Radegund, circa 520–587, whose friend Bishop Venantius Fortunatus wrote hymns—still used in church liturgy—to celebrate the arrival of the relic gift. The Ottonian emperors at the turn of the millennium were also recipients of generous gifts. Indeed, True Cross relics, even those held by ecclesiastical institutions, came to be especially associated with royal ownership or donation. Other kings and emperors, such as the Spanish Asturian kings and the Carolingian emperors (Charlemagne in the eighth century as well as Charles the Bald in the ninth), were also reputed to have possessed and, in turn, gifted relics of the True Cross, although the provenance of some these relics, known only from historical sources, is not entirely clear.[37]

Exchanges of relics of the True Cross during the early medieval period, although often well documented and of great historical consequence, were completely eclipsed by the massive movement of True Cross relics that began with the onset of the Crusades. It is no surprise that, for a Crusader, one of the most coveted rewards for sacrifice and service was a relic of the True Cross. The Crusades, in fact, were pursued in the name of and under the sign of the cross. As Cecilia Gaposchkin has demonstrated, the liturgy of departure involved a pilgrim's blessing that was supplemented with the bestowal and blessing of a cross insignia upon the Crusader. The ceremony emphasized the personal relationship of the soldier with the cross, showing he was to take up the cross in imitation of Christ.[38] In calling for the Crusades, Pope Urban II urged, "Let the cross glitter on your arms and on your standards . . . [on your] shoulders . . . and . . . breasts . . . [as] emblem of victory or palm of martyrdom."[39] Once again we are struck by the multivalent quality of the cross and its unique and inordinate power for Christians, a quality highlighted by Thomas Aquinas in the *Summa Theologica* (1265–1274): "We worship the image of Christ's cross in any material."[40]

Thus, although other Passion relics, such as the thorns from the Crown of Thorns were also much desired during the Crusades, relics of the Cross were voraciously acquired by the victors. A chart from the important study by Anatole Frolow on the True Cross relics shows the sudden increase of relics in the West after the Crusades, especially after the Sack of Constantinople in 1204.[41] From about fifty texts attesting to relics in the West before the year 1000, the number of documents testifying to separate relics of the True Cross peaks at more than two hundred in the thirteenth century. The True Cross relic of the Venetian Scuola Grande di San Giovanni Evangelista, discussed at the opening of this chapter, was a highly significant Crusader gift, donated in 1369 by Philip de Mezières, chancellor of the Kingdom of Jerusalem and the Kingdom of Cyprus. Even the Crusader-king Louis IX did not consider his collection, intended for his palace chapel in Paris (discussed further in chapter 2), to be complete until he received his relic of the True Cross; the arrival of the relic was cause for massive public ceremonies, which were depicted in the thirteenth-century chronicles of the English monk Matthew Paris (fig. 13).

Matthew's drawing reveals a new form for the cross in this era. Rather than resembling what is called the Latin cross with its long upright, or the equal-armed Greek cross, or even the five-fold Crusader cross (a new heraldic form), this cross can be recognized by its extra horizontal crosspiece. Today often called the Patriarchal or Orthodox cross, it may derive its shape, with the

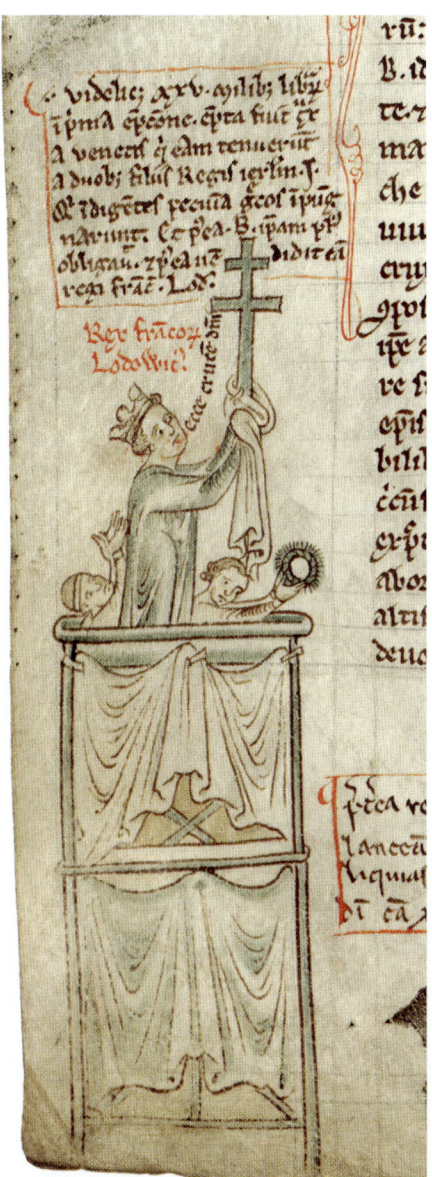

Figure 13. "Public Showing of the True Cross Relic by Louis IX," in Matthew Paris, *Chronica Maiora II*, CCCC MS 16, fol. 142v, 13th century. Vellum manuscript, 35.8 × 24.4 cm. Parker Library, Corpus Christi College, Cambridge. (Photo: © Parker Library, Corpus Christi College)

additional smaller upper horizontal crosspiece, from representations of the *Titulus*, or title board. This shape became common in the East beginning in the tenth century and, given that most Eastern reliquaries take this form, it serves as a marker for the power of the relic of the True Cross coming from the East.[42]

Crusader treasures of the True Cross came primarily from Constantinople, as is the case with Louis's cross, and it was important that any new owner demonstrate the authenticity and therefore the provenance of his relic in its presentation—that is, its reliquary. From an earlier period of the Crusades, in commissioning the beautiful Stavelot Triptych (now in the Morgan Museum and Library), Abbot Wibald included two diminutive reliquary triptychs in the center of the ensemble to display True Cross relics he had obtained on a diplomatic mission to Constantinople. In the creation of these two embedded triptychs, Wibald presented objects with an appearance so convincingly "Byzantine" that they fool many modern viewers (see fig. 2). In this case, the Eastern iconography and art techniques of reused, assembled fragments (cloisonné enamel panels versus the champlevé of the rest of the reliquary) proclaim the Eastern origins of the relics. More typically, patrons and artists use the double-armed Eastern cross shape to make the visual argument that a relic is authentic.

The Crusaders' importation of relics is arguably the most important chapter of the history of the relic of the True Cross. It is the moment to which we can trace the proliferation of relics in the West, the expansion of the use of the cross in political insignia—both Crusader emblems and heraldry—and the beginning of the practice of devotion to the *Arma Christi* (to be discussed in the next chapter). It spurred veneration of the other Passion relics and resulted in the manufacture of many new reliquaries and chapels. Consideration of one example from among these many Crusader riches will help us understand the complex issues of cross reliquaries—their manufacture, dissemination, and use in this period.

## JERUSALEM CROSSES AND THE TOULOUSE CHÂSSE

The so-called Jerusalem crosses (fig. 14), mentioned briefly above, are small but significant examples of the sort of object desired by Crusaders as a testament to victory and virtue. They were made exclusively during the period of the Latin Kingdom of Jerusalem (1099–1187), in the city of Jerusalem itself. In addition to relics of the True Cross, the "gems" that decorate these crosses, rather than the usual precious or semiprecious sort, are stones taken from sites in the Holy Land; the body of the crosses are made of silver and gilded silver over a wood core. With the addition of the supplementary location relics, the crosses were able to serve as a sort of self-contained and condensed spiritual pilgrimage and witness to the sacred geography of the Holy Land. Also called Crusader crosses, the approximately ten surviving examples are considered very small for ceremonial crosses. Rather than having been intended for a spectacular effect in a procession, they seem to have been made to be held in the hand, creating an intimate relationship with a devotee.[43] The desirability of the form is witnessed by the copies of these crosses that were made in European workshops (fig. 15).

Although some of these crosses may have been commissioned by Western prelates and kings, others originated as gifts from institutions in the Latin Kingdom of Jerusalem to Western churches and monasteries, and their histories and usage are documented in some instances. The Denkendorf cross (fig. 14) was a gift of the Patriarch of Jerusalem to a pilgrim who in turn gifted it as the foundation object for a monastery that had been awarded privileges by Pope Honorius III in 1128.[44] Another example, the Scheyern cross, is still preserved with a document that suggests that it should serve as a substitute for pilgrimage for those who could not travel.[45] The Denkendorf cross and others, including examples in Barlatta and Conques, attest to their Jerusalem origin with a tiny image of the Holy Sepulcher at the base of the cross (see fig. 14).

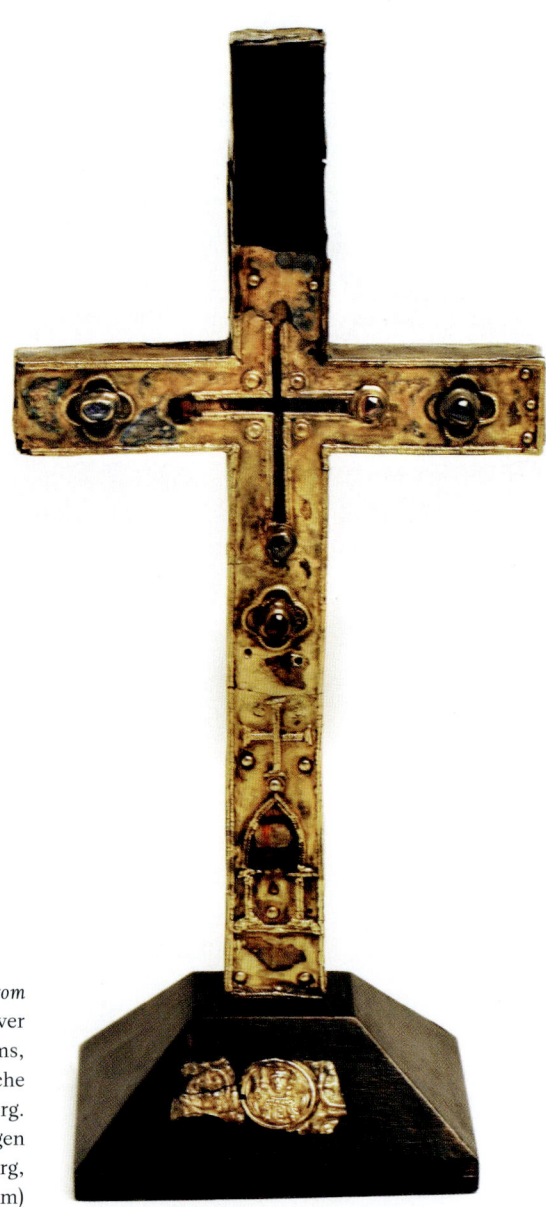

Figure 14. *Jerusalem Cross from Denkendorf*, c. 1135. Wood, silver with gilding, and gems, 20.5 × 10.6 × 1.4 cm. Städtische Kunstsammlungen, Augsburg. (Photo: © Kunstsammlungen und Museen Augsburg, Maximilianmuseum)

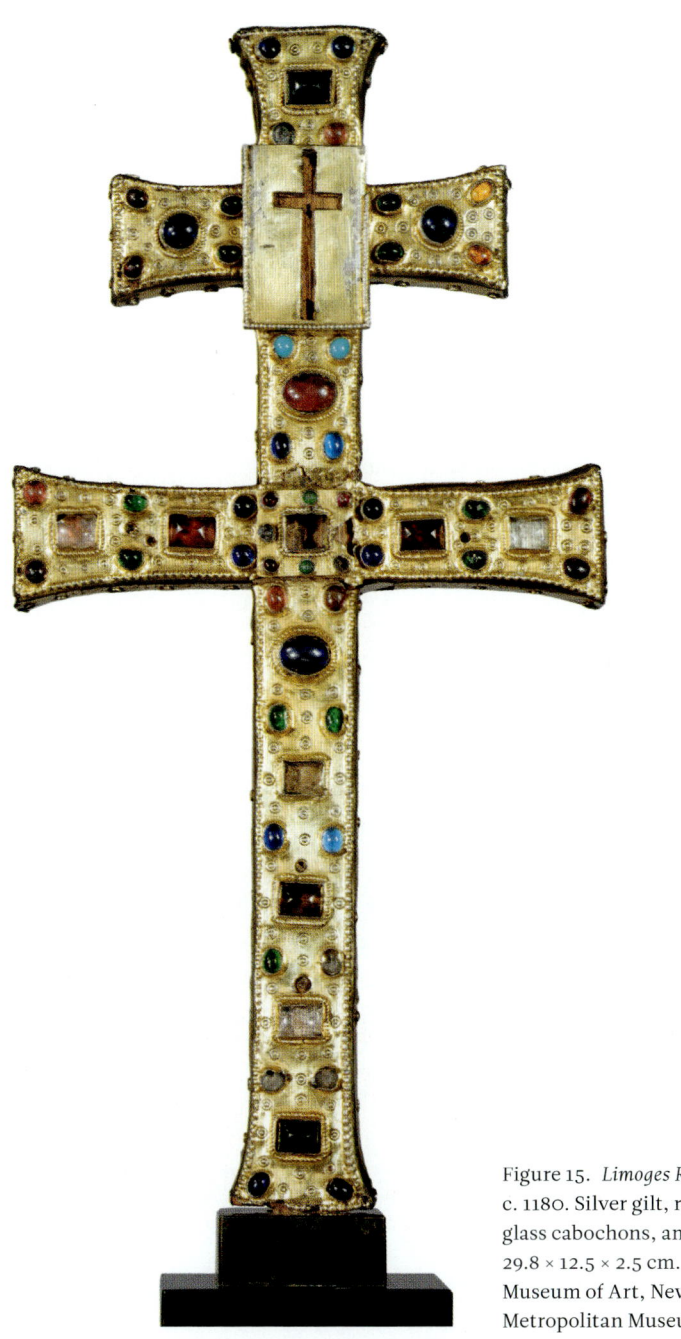

Figure 15. *Limoges Reliquary Cross*, c. 1180. Silver gilt, rock crystal, glass cabochons, and wood core, 29.8 × 12.5 × 2.5 cm. Metropolitan Museum of Art, New York. (Photo: Metropolitan Museum of Art)

For our purposes, however, the most interesting and informative story about one of the Crusader crosses involves a cross that no longer survives. The history of the Toulouse cross is preserved in a narrative recorded in images on a Limoges reliquary made to contain it in circa 1178–1198 and today preserved in the treasury of Saint-Sernin.[46] I should note that larger reliquaries made to hold cross-shaped True Cross reliquaries have been common since the earliest era. Famously, Radegund's relic of the Cross was secured in a cross-shaped reliquary and further deposited in a larger ceremonial box, and a similar double reliquary enclosed an important Vatican Cross relic.[47]

The Limoges reliquary was meant to serve as the repository of the now lost Jerusalem cross and details the journey of the cross reliquary in a pictorial history that gives us indications of both the use and of the meaning of the object, beginning with a sort of provenance or origin story (figs. 16–18).[48] This sort of specificity, with multiple narrative episodes and explanatory inscriptions, is highly unusual in Limoges enamel reliquary production, or on any reliquary for that matter.

On the short end of the châsse (fig. 16), the discovery of the True Cross in Jerusalem by Saint Helena is depicted as proof of the relic's origin and importance. On one long side (fig. 17), we are witness to a very specific ceremony, the gift of a relic of the Cross, now enclosed in a distinctively Eastern double-arm reliquary. The cross is being donated by Abbas De Iosaphat (the abbot of Our Lady of Josaphat in the Kidron Valley, the location of Mary's Tomb) to a representative from Toulouse. That representative, also identified in a label, Raymond Botardelli, is a historical figure known as a scribe at Saint-Sernin. Raymond accepts the cross with the speech act inscribed on a scroll:

Figure 16. "Helena Discovering the True Cross," *Reliquary of the True Cross* (side view), 1178–98. Gilded copper and champlevé enamel, 13 × 29.2 × 14 cm. Basilique Saint-Sernin, Musée Saint-Raymond, Toulouse. (Photo: © Jean-François Peiré—DRAC Occitanie)

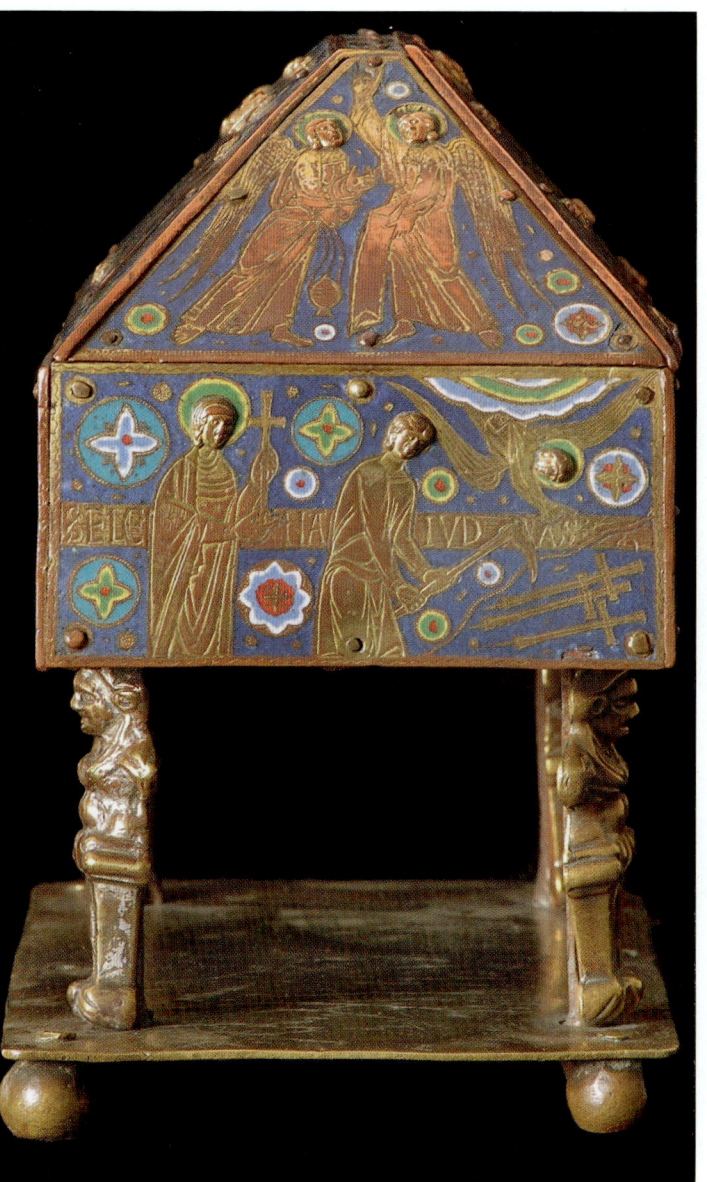

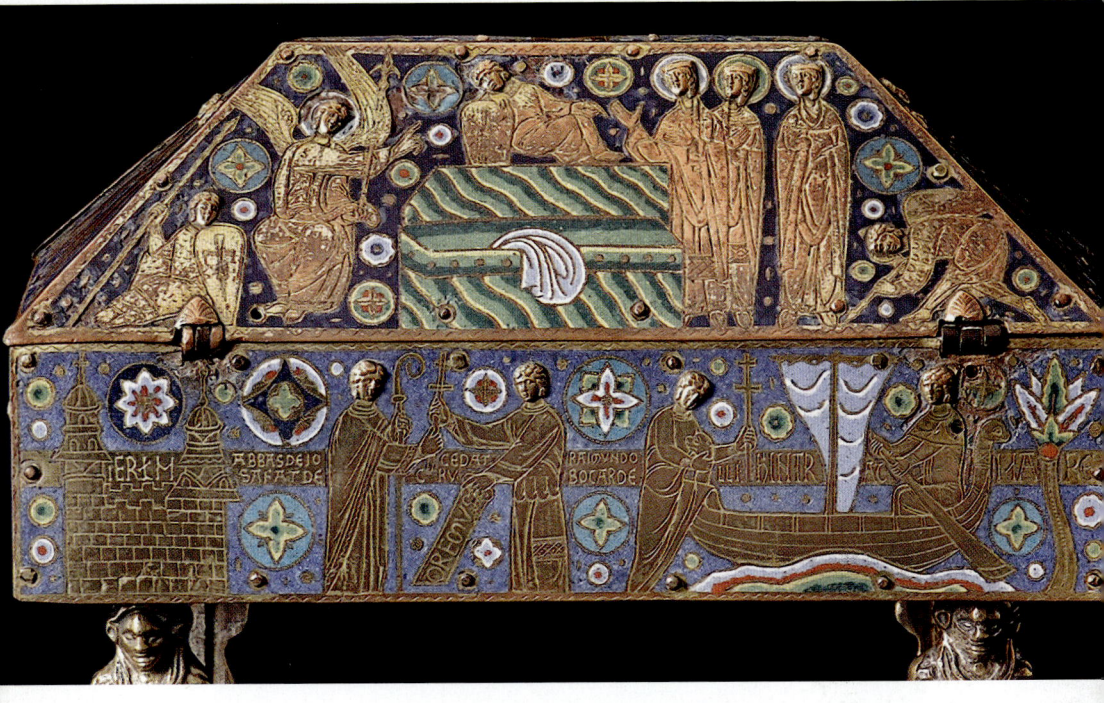

Figure 17. "Marys at the Tomb and Scenes of the Donation of a Cross," *Reliquary of the True Cross*, 1178–98. (Photo: © Jean-François Peiré—DRAC Occitanie)

"OREMUS" (Let us pray), thus placing the cross within the realm of holy action and quite literally situating it in networks of prayerful exchange and reception.[49] Immediately upon accomplishing the goal of his pilgrimage to Jerusalem, Raymond returns by ship to Toulouse, and in the next scene, on the other short end of the reliquary, offers the cross to Abbot Pons of Saint-Sernin, who blesses him.

The formal acceptance and completion of the narrative, however, does not occur until, on the other long side of the châsse (fig. 18), the official liturgical celebrants of the abbey come out of the church to receive the cross in a

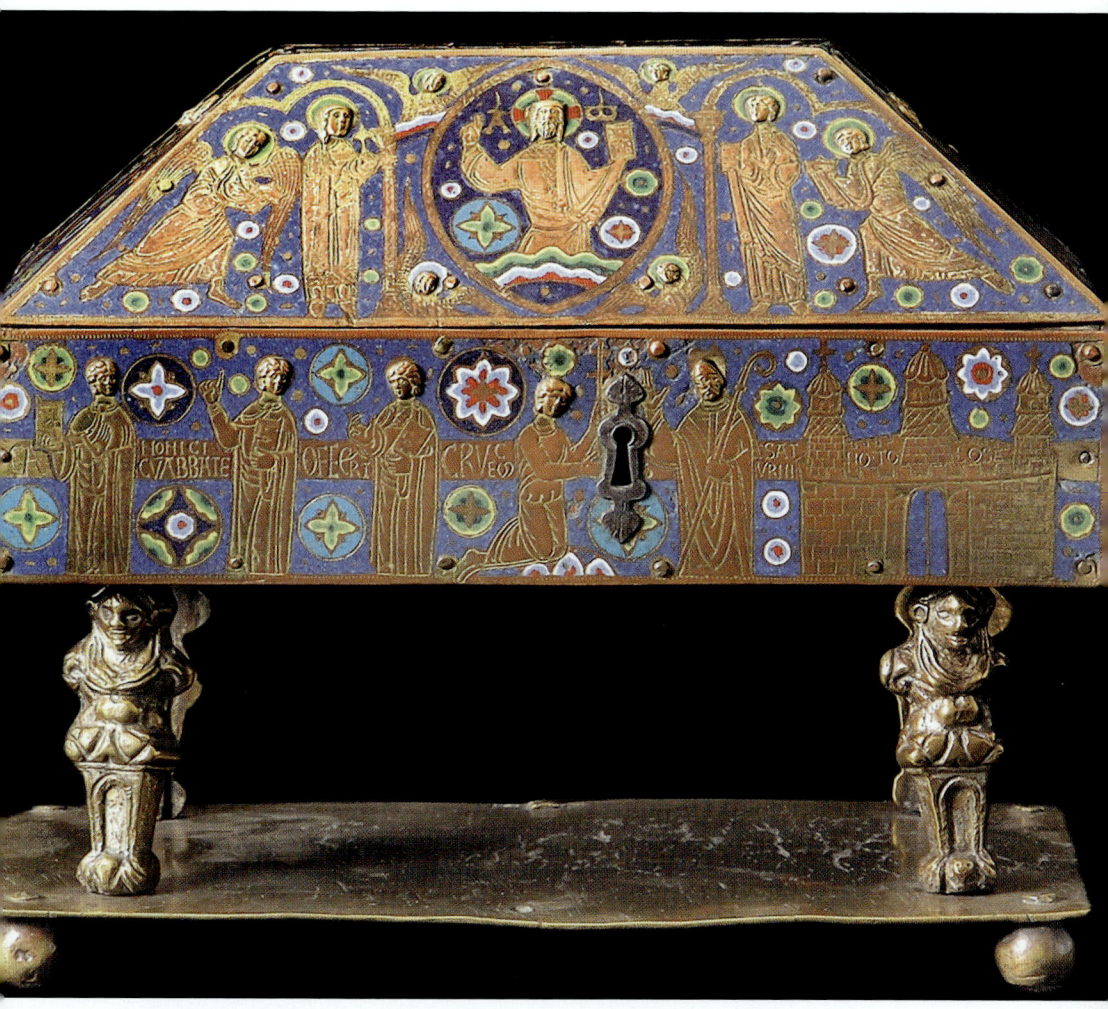

Figure 18. "Majestas (Rev. 12:15–19) and Further Scenes of the Donation of a Cross," *Reliquary of the True Cross*, 1178–98. (Photo: © Jean-François Peiré—DRAC Occitanie)

kind of *adventus*. The *Adventus* ceremony, modeled on the Roman imperial staging to welcome an emperor to a city, was modified in the early medieval period to suit the advent or translation of relics.[50] In this scene of the châsse, the foremost celebrants move out of the church/city holding ceremonial objects (that is, books) and making gestures of welcome. In a form of medieval simultaneous narrative, Raymond has already passed them and, on bended knee, proffers the cross to the abbot. The abbot responds with a gesture of welcome (rather spoiled by the later addition of the lock to the châsse). The inscription emphasizes that the depicted canons and abbot in turn offer the cross to Saint-Sernin, making them the agents of the gift and of the prayers and benefits it entails. Thus, the city of Toulouse receives the cross as a sort of arriving figure of royalty, which has traveled forth from Jerusalem and entered Toulouse, gracing its new home with its presence and divinity. This is significant transfer of holy power.

It should not be forgotten that Toulouse (here shown as powerful city of three towers and an open gate, pictured in precisely the same way both on the reliquary and on the seal of the Count) was one of the foremost cities of southern France, the capital of its county, and an important stop for travelers on the pilgrimage road to Santiago; its rulers intermarried with royalty and were vastly wealthy and powerful. Count Raymond IV of Toulouse, one of the first and most renowned leaders of the Crusades, was the source of significant relic gifts to the church from the Holy Land in the early twelfth century, and Saint-Sernin was even reputed to have once received gifts from Charlemagne. One scholar has indeed compared Raymond IV's reputation to that of Charlemagne—both men visited both Jerusalem and Constantinople and brought back precious relic gifts.[51] This relic of the True Cross as well as its container would have been a welcome addition to the church's already prestigious collection.

Perhaps it should come as no surprise that some of the earliest monumental sculptures of the Romanesque period had been created for this site and its treasury almost a hundred years before the True Cross relic arrived. Inventories register a steady accumulation of relics that drew attention to the Toulouse, and the church treasury. Although the treasury and the city itself as the capital of a county would be significantly diminished as a result of the Albigensian Crusade against the Cathar heresy—a military campaign principally fought between 1209 and 1215 and concluded by King Louis IX, which destroyed the political independence of the region and integrated it into the French kingdom—the magnitude of Toulouse's earlier medieval glory should not be ignored.

If we look to the rest of the imagery on the reliquary box, commissioned in the last years of Toulouse's medieval grandeur, perhaps we can put the reception of the relic cross in a more complete context. We can try to understand how the medieval audience would have understood the imagery especially in its ceremonial and monumental environment.

Above the scene of the gift of the cross passed to Raymond in Jerusalem, the imagery of the Marys at the Tomb is depicted on the roof of the châsse (fig. 17). Thinking liturgically rather than in terms of story or history (as Raymond's speech act on the reliquary has already encouraged us to do), this depiction of the empty tomb recalls the contemporary practice of the liturgical dramatization of this scene, the *Visitatio Sepulchri*. In preparation for that drama, the cross was buried in the week preceding the Easter Ceremony. On Easter, the cross would then be ceremonially lifted from the grave as a dramatization of the Resurrection. A core part of the first portion of the drama, customarily performed by three clerics playing the part of the Marys, was the *Quem Quaeritis* (Whom do you seek?) trope—that is, the question the angel asked the Marys. This trope originated in the tenth century as did the subsequent *Elevatio* ceremony in which the cross (or sometimes a host) was lifted from its burial place in the "Sepulcher." These liturgical performances were increasingly common in the twelfth century, when this casket was made, and indeed were even celebrated in liturgies in Jerusalem in the Holy Sepulcher itself.[52]

Frescoes variously dated from 1118 to 1180 were uncovered in the 1970s next to a door opening to a stair to the gallery level of Saint-Sernin. The frescoes, like the casket, depict the Three Marys visiting the Tomb, and an angel is "perched" above the door as if it were the entrance to the tomb. These frescoes have been seen as evidence of performance of the theatrical *Quem Quaeritis* liturgy in this location in the church.[53] If the reliquary box was used to "entomb" the Jerusalem cross, this door and stair space may have been used to further "bury" the châsse. If so, we may see the imagery of the Marys more generally in a context of the Easter celebration, which would include a culminating scene (as in the frescoes and also on the châsse) depicting the resurrected Christ as king reigning in the Celestial Temple (the vision of Rev. 12:15-19). Iconographic parallels between the reliquary and the frescoes are indeed striking: both include the scene at the Tomb and a heavenly vision. Both also feature a separation and emphasis on the soldiers who guard the Tomb. This emphasis on the soldiers merits a closer look.[54]

On the châsse, in particular, rather than the somnolent, unaware Roman soldiers typical of the *Visitatio* scene, we see markedly alert and attentive Crusader soldiers, all of whom carry shields marked with crosses. One of soldiers, at the far left, turns toward the tomb holding both a spear and a shield inscribed with the cross fitchée—that is, a combination of cross and sword, easy to fix in the ground and associated with Crusaders.[55] A second soldier on the châsse bows deeply towards the tomb and the Marys, touching his spear to the ground at their feet and wearing the cross on his "shoulder" on his shield. A third, above the tomb and between the other two, seems to participate in the series of gestures that knits the scene together—the angel points, the Crusader relays the message, and the foremost Mary gratefully receives the "good news." As a group, the three perform acts of protection, mediation, and prayer. Finally, at least one of the soldiers has bare feet as if depicted as respectful of holy ground. The change in the iconography of the soldiers from asleep to alert decisively diverts it from the historical perception of Roman military overlords controlling the tomb through a show of force and unaware of its significance, portraying instead the protective role of the Crusaders in Latin Jerusalem.

Such a depiction of sympathetic soldiers at the Tomb of Christ is almost unprecedented in medieval and Renaissance art and literature. I have found only a few other instances that show exceptions to the rule. Two are English and late Medieval: the first is liturgical evidence that English parish churches used the role of the soldiers as a major focus of lay participation in "protecting" the contents of the tomb while the cross was buried from Good Friday until Easter Monday;[56] the second is a fifteenth-century English alabaster in the Victoria and Albert Museum that shows attentive witnessing soldiers.[57] Only one example is close to contemporary to the Toulouse reliquary. An ivory tower reliquary in the Victoria and Albert Museum, circa 1180 from Cologne and with possible Jerusalem and Crusader connections, features a *Visitatio* that doubles the number of soldiers. Three are helmed and dressed in mail and asleep. The other three soldiers are dressed in cloaks like those on the Toulouse casket and are awake.[58]

Thus, a further context for the extraordinary iconographic revisionism of the Toulouse châsse should be sought in Jerusalem as well as in the key role that Toulouse and its leaders played in the history of the Crusades.

We should recall that Raymond, count of Toulouse (d. 1105), was among the wealthiest, most senior, and most important early leaders of the Crusades, and he was, according to a chronicler in his entourage, very pious.[59] He traveled with the papal legate, Adhemar, bishop of Le Puy (d. 1098), and his role in the siege of Antioch was an early high point of his Crusade experience. His men arrived at the city first and were the cohort that eventually prevailed in the siege. They did so, however, in a contest that was not wholly military but centered instead on certain extraordinary and influential events—initiated by the discovery of a renowned relic, the holy lance.

The sequence of events began when a peasant monk in Raymond's entourage, Peter Bartholomew, experienced a series of visions during the siege. In the first, he was led into the city of Antioch by the Apostle Andrew and shown a precious relic—the lance that had pierced Christ's side. Saint Andrew urged him to tell Count Raymond and to return after the capture of the city to find the relic. The monk was also instructed that the Crusaders should process around the city barefoot as penance in order to deserve a victory. Peter's reports of his visions heartened the Crusaders; they followed the saintly instructions, were able to capture the city, and retrieved the lance relic. (The lance is further discussed in chapter 2, and its discovery in Antioch is illustrated in fig. 29.)

In contrast, the papal legate Adhemar was somewhat skeptical about the visions and the relic. The Germans and the Normans, especially Arnulf of Chocques (d. 1118), openly mocked Peter and even challenged the authenticity of the lance. Despite the pious reception of the relic by Raymond's entourage—wrapping it in cloths that had been soaked in the Jordan, performing ceremonies of kissing and processing, crediting it with help in the siege[60]—it may be that the low status of the monk who experienced the visions undermined the willingness of the Crusaders outside of Raymond's circle to accept the relic's legitimacy. Peter was finally forced to test the relic: he volunteered to walk on burning coals carrying the lance, putting it, in effect, to trial by fire. He made the walk to great acclaim but died twelve days later of injuries. Raymond was so furious about Arnulf's role in the affair that he sent soldiers to hunt him down, but Arnulf was protected by other factions. The relic itself was eventually lost.

Successive events are perhaps of even greater interest for what we could term the material culture of the piety of the Crusades. Following the success of the relic of the lance in inspiring the soldiers, Arnulf of Chocques and the bishop of Martirano had a golden image of Christ made to be placed on Godfrey of Bouillon's siege engine during the subsequent siege of Jerusalem.

Soon after the Crusaders captured the holy city, the discovery of a much more significant relic was made. Like the lance, it was excavated from the very earth of the Holy Land and quickly put to use in inspiring the Crusader forces.

Arnulf "discovered" a relic of the True Cross hidden "probably in the 'garden' of the Holy Sepulcher compound."[61] Undoubtedly because of his political connections, superior ability to implement church ceremony and traditions, and higher clerical status—as the first patriarch of Latin Crusader Jerusalem[62]—Arnulf succeeded where Peter Bartholomew had failed. The True Cross relic became a new and potent battle standard for the Crusaders and became a central focus of devotion in the Holy Sepulcher.

Arnulf also found other ways to use the power of the relic of the True Cross to great effect. He reorganized the Holy Sepulcher and its services, ousted the Orthodox clerics who had previously controlled the shrine, and instituted canons on the Western model, establishing a Latin Crusader liturgy. He was able to win monetary support for a monastery of the Cross established at the Holy Sepulcher, and other monasteries were endowed via Crusader funds throughout Jerusalem. The Holy Sepulcher was rebuilt (completed much later, in 1149, under Queen Melisende, placing all the associated holy sites of the area under one roof), as were the Church of the Nativity and many other buildings, including the church at the monastery of Our Lady in Josaphat, where the Tomb of Mary was located. In a version of the Byzantine name, the Anastasis, Crusaders began calling the Church of the Holy Sepulcher the Church of the Resurrection and emphasized the links between the earthly and the heavenly Jerusalem. Processions, liturgies, and prayer brotherhoods connected the holy sites during this time, as Jerusalem was turned into a spectacular performance arena for the holy.

Not satisfied with the amplification of sanctity in Jerusalem itself, the Crusaders brought their new Holy Land liturgical celebrations home with them. Just as in Jerusalem, in many Western churches the Easter liturgy was repeated and recast as a feast on July 15 that celebrated the liberation of Jerusalem. In one such celebration at Ripoll, Crusader chronicles were read, and a sermon addressed to a lay audience praised the "soldiers" as heroes, exulting that there were no longer enemy guards at the gates of Jerusalem.[63] Liturgies characterized the pious actions of the Crusaders, intoning that "[the cross] sign is held high" and "honor is . . . rendered to the tomb."[64] The Order of the Sepulcher was founded and dependent monasteries were established in locations as diverse as Barcelona and Paris. Members of the order, including not only ecclesiastics but also knights and members of the nobility, prayed for one another. The surviving sixteenth-century necrology in Barcelona includes names from across Spain as well as from Jerusalem and Montpellier.[65]

It is in this context that we should understand the material objects that survive. The so-called Jerusalem crosses represent relics of the True Cross but also include the tiny stones that derive from other locations particularly celebrated by the Crusaders, such as the Church of the Nativity, the Holy Sepulcher, and Calvary. Recall that the Scheyern cross was offered as a substitute for pilgrimage and the Denkendorf, Barlatta, and Conques crosses bear an image of the Sepulcher (see fig. 14, bottom of the shaft). Clearly these little relic crosses had outsize importance as representatives of the spaces and powers of the Holy Land.

Ultimately, on the Limoges châsse the story of the True Cross relic and its journey to Toulouse is retold not as an instance of historical documentation but as an important and integral episode in the history of Salvation. On what I would like to see as the primary face of the Toulouse châsse, the upper scene of the *Majestas Domini* fulfills the vision of Revelation that follows the seventh trumpet (see fig. 18). The image emphasizes Christ's kingship in the Heavenly Jerusalem; therefore, Christ reigns over and sanctions the sacred translation of the cross to Toulouse. Jerusalem is marked with a special grace as the location of the tomb of the Lord, but its power can be and is relocated with the translation of the relic to Toulouse through the agency not of its count, but of the canons of Saint-Sernin. We witness the solemnity of the transfer of the holy from one site to another, the cross "held high," carried from the closed walls of Jerusalem to the welcoming wide-open doors of "Tolosa," from the Sacred Tomb of Christ revealed to the three Marys and "honored" and protected by devout soldiers of the Crusades. Finally it arrives at the new center of sanctity and is received by the three celebrants who perform in place of the holy women as witnesses to the Resurrection.

The reliquary châsse thus imparts a complex story to its audience about the many dimensions of the significance of the cross. In this story the cross plays a role not only as a relic but also as a repository of social exchange. It is a sign of sacred history and sacred place, but it is also an object that can be held, kissed, ceremonially processed, and venerated. A discussion of this one small but sumptuous object has served as a remarkable summation to this discussion of the multivalence and theatricality of the cross. In that it tells the history of a cross as the special focus of veneration for a community, it also demonstrates that although there were many crosses, each might have its own worth, its own story.

One last episode can close our story about the striking success of the Crusaders in focusing devotion on the cross and solidifying the power of the relic of the True Cross as the inspiration for both crusading soldiers and European devotees. A history of the conquest of Jerusalem and the capture in 1187 of the "Great Cross" (that is, Arnulf's relic), written by a Muslim, supplies another remarkably vivid image of the power of the cross for its Christian audience:

> When the priests exposed it to view and the heads [of the bearers] bore it along all would run and cast themselves down around it, and no one was allowed to lag behind or hang back without forfeiting his liberty. . . . They fainted at its appearance, they raised their eyes to contemplate it, they were consumed with passion when it was exhibited and boasted of nothing else when they

had seen it. They went into ecstasies at its reappearance, they offered up their lives for it and sought comfort from it, so much so that they had copies made of it which they worshipped, before which they prostrated themselves in their houses and on which they called when they gave evidence.[66]

The Muslim author derides the required response—no one is allowed to "lag behind or hang back"—but his evidence also testifies to the ability of the relic and the Latin Church to create a unity of response among its devotees. It was this response, however, that also laid the foundation of the Crusaders' defeat. When the cross was captured by Saladin, "great was the calamity that befell [the Christian Crusaders], and the strength drained from their loins."[67] The cross of Jerusalem was never recovered, and the Crusader project never again met with the success of the First Crusade.

In conclusion, as we have worked our way through a series of crosses, many of which were reliquary crosses, we have learned much about the complex nature of the cross and the staging of the True Cross relic in the Middle Ages. From the lavish to the seemingly simple, from emblem of punishment to that of victory, from material cross—although a material that fluctuates and changes—to object of narrative, drama, and poetry, we are surely astonished by the range of this thing, this sign. We have seen that the cross of the Middle Ages is a concept that is only fully realized as a performance. In its interactions and revisualizations, in its many manifestations in every part of the world and every part of life, it moves through time and space as thing and not-thing, as insistently material and yet "purely" semiotic, but always powerful. The cross is embedded in ritual, in prayer, and in programs of sensual interaction that during the Middle Ages continually reinforce its physical nature—all while living most vividly in the imagination. As the "Dream of the Rood" proclaimed, it is ultimately the cross that marks the Christian's path to salvation: "Through the cross every soul who desires to dwell with the Lord shall come to the Kingdom."

CHAPTER TWO

# Passion Relics

*Strength in Unity*

### INSTRUMENTS OF TORTURE

The cross, even today, remains the charged and changeable field upon which the body of Christ is imagined, displayed, tortured, and venerated. In contrast, the other instruments of the Passion exemplify aggression against that body. Wielded by Christ's enemies, as the active elements in the Passion narrative, precisely because they are the instruments that cause his suffering, the objects used to torment Christ become material testimony. In their form as holy relics, they witness to his divinity and to his kingship, but above all to his humanity

As Elaine Scarry has so eloquently argued, we cannot effectively imagine pain without imagining the tools that inflict pain.[1] The primary Passion relics are those tools Christians use to imaginatively enter the events of the Passion in order that they might achieve empathy and the "blessed" tears of compunction and salvation. Indeed, although the implements all appear as part of the narrative of the Gospel story, their purported and extraordinary preservation as material objects seems to be due to a religious need for the concrete manifestation of instruments of empathetic response—even if the inescapable emotional effect on devotees is sorrow and pain.

Unlike the early manifestation of the cult of the True Cross, the cults of the various relics of the Passion arrive later in the Middle Ages. Some of the Passion relics achieved renown, it would seem, as a response to the great campaigns of relic collecting in pursuit of royal or imperial status, beginning as early as the Carolingian period and culminating during and after the Crusades. Others were venerated spontaneously when devotion to the suffering of Christ was developing as a religious practice, primarily in the thirteenth century and later. Whatever their origins might be, Passion relics proved to be immensely powerful for believers, especially in terms of their somatic affect. Although not parts of any body, it cannot be denied that they still most insistently reference corporeality and evoke bodily response.

Even before the great era of Passion relics of the later Middle Ages, already in the early Middle Ages the True Cross set the standards of response to such relics. The cross can, as we have seen, make specific, imaginative demands upon the viewer's body. It can be said to urge the mind to contemplate its hard surfaces and compel the body to conform to its harsh shape in what can be construed as a conventional, yet rapt response. Or in another mode, the cross is cast as active and itself body-like: it has arms and legs and a measure comparable to the body and it is frequently referred to as living. Similarly Passion relics create myriad imaginative and productive effects on the body: the nails can pierce the hands and feet, the crown can circle and frame the head, and the sacred cloths can wrap the body. Additionally, as we will see, they, too, can act as if they were alive.

Finally, their materials are of particular interest. The great compendium of sacred stories, the *Golden Legend* (c. 1270 and later) lingers on a description of the wood of Calvary before the Crucifixion, describing it as a sterile, dark, ignoble, even "malodorous" material that is transformed through its use as the Cross to a valuable, fertile, light-giving, even sublime substance.[2] In similar insistent material presence and effect, other Passion relics are stubbornly material and those materials are credited with wondrous powers.

In this chapter, in investigating Passion relics we will first consider texts: Biblical, historical, and devotional, many of which predate any evidence of surviving objects. Although we will be much engaged in thinking of the relics as a group, it will be helpful to locate and discuss a selection of individual relics as they are purported to survive in church treasuries. In subsequently turning to the great collections of Passion relics that were made across Europe, we will come to understand why such collections were considered to support political power. Finally, we will consider the interrelation of the relics with devotions to the body and suffering of Christ, especially as witnessed by the creation of the notion of the *Arma Christi*.

In 1870 the architect and gentleman archaeologist Charles Rohault de Fleury wrote an ambitious summary of the stories, origins, and locations of Passion relics.[3] In his introductory letter, Pope Pius IX promised that the publication of this treatise with its "scientific" approach would quell ridicule and respond to Protestant objections to relics. Rohault de Fleury's approach both rationalized the multiplications and disparities among examples of any given relic and provided careful drawings and assessments of surviving objects (fig. 19).[4] Many in the Catholic Church, in any mention of these relics, still echo his conclusions. For example, Rohault de Fleury explained that the majority of surviving thorn relics were derived from a particular plant from the Holy Land with very long spines—the *Zizyphus spina-christi*—rather than from the more common European thorn depicted in many images that date from the Middle Ages.[5] He also argued that the Crown sat on Christ's head as a kind of helmet, with arching elements over the head. This material explanation still prevails in discussion of the relic of the Crown that survives in Notre-Dame in Paris.

The French scholar not only examined and assembled documents about all the known Passion relics, but he also attempted to put the relics in a general hierarchy, following a similar urge to classify that we have seen with the relics of the True Cross. For example, he calls the nails "the greatest treasure

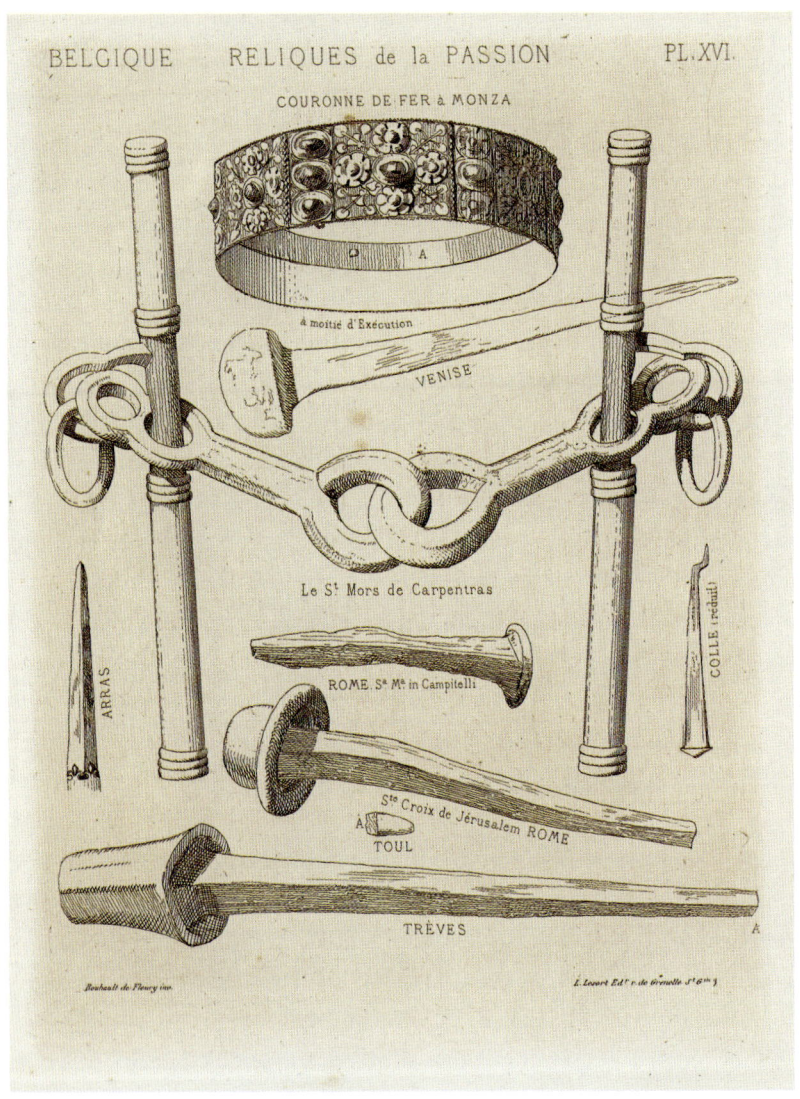

Figure 19. Holy Nails, in Charles Rohault de Fleury, *Mémoire sur les instruments de la passion de N.-S. J.-C.*, plate XVI, published 1870. Ingalls Library, Cleveland Museum of Art. (Photo: Ingalls Library, Cleveland Museum of Art)

after the cross,"[6] because they entered Christ's body and were stained with his blood (see fig. 19). Nevertheless, he gives the nails scant treatment in contrast to his long discussion of the Crown of Thorns. It may be that he preferred the Crown because it was a great national treasure of his homeland.

Even if they are often venerated, discussed singly, and ranked against one another, Passion relics tend to appear in groups. In order to add luster to their rule, kings and emperors avidly collected as many of these sacred objects as possible. There is no denying that the relics were and are more powerful as a group, but the reason for this collective potency is not at first entirely obvious.

One explanation is theological and liturgical. Even in the earliest discussions of the Passion, Christ's body is discussed as "broken" and metaphorically dismembered through his torture by his persecutors and the instruments of the Passion; nevertheless, his body is then in a sense reassembled.[7] In this imagery, Christ's sacrifice is compared to Jewish sacrificial practices of the "bruising" or "breaking in pieces" of the sacrifice (Isa. 53:7 and 10, Lev. 2:5–6), in reference to the lamb or grain sacrifice. Such breaking of course should be compared to the Eucharist (1 Cor. 11:24): "And when he had given thanks, he brake *it*, and said, Take, eat: this is my body, which is broken for you: this do in remembrance of me." At the same time that dismemberment of the sacrifice is a central Judeo-Christian principle, however, the reconsolidation and inventory of the *unbroken* body of Christ is essential to the Christian faith. Christ is a willing sacrifice, but he is also God. John Lansdowne has shown how the Byzantine Orthodox rite vividly reenacts this essential paradox of "broken but not divided" in the Eucharistic service.[8]

One other all-important aspect of the Passion story is essential to understanding the collective power of Passion relics. Unlike most narratives of torture and death, the Passion story ends in victory and resurrection. The ending reorients all that comes before, thus allowing the instruments of torture to become not only the means of division but also the means of consolidation and consolation. The consolation of the end of the story is at the heart of veneration and devotion to the instruments of the Passion. It helps explain how implements of torture and pain came to be central objects in Christian religion—and became so significant to the political aspirations of monarchs.

The Apocryphal Acts of Thomas, dating from the first quarter of the third century and undoubtedly reflecting early Christian liturgical understanding, is early evidence of this sort of paradoxical transformation of the instruments and their use in spiritual and devotional thought. It also, like other early textual and pictorial examples, stands emphatically apart from any evidence of material relics. The text lists Christ's torments and their instrumental means, enumerating how contemplation of and interaction with each could strengthen or heal the Christian: "Thine *holy body* which was crucified for us do *we eat*, and *thy blood* that was shed for us unto salvation do *we drink*; let therefore thy body be unto us salvation and thy blood for remission of sins. And for *the gall which thou didst drink* for our sakes let *the gall of the devil be removed* from us: and for *the vinegar which thou hast drunk* for us, let our weakness be made strong: and for *the spitting which thou didst receive* for us, *let us receive the dew of thy goodness*" (italics added).[9] From this list of materials—especially liquids to be ingested—the text continues with the objects of ridicule and torture—the reed, crown, and linen cloth. Just as the imagined fluid exchange transforms the Christian, gall and vinegar cleansing him or her of sin and weakness, spittle returned as the dew of forgiveness, the other Passion materials, such as the crown and linen cloth, wrap and comfort the Christian. The tomb is invoked as a final comfort and enclosure.

A tenth-century Byzantine ivory shows a second approach to understanding the possibilities of the instruments of the Passion and seems to reflect another early Christian text. In this text, the instruments are gathered as a means of defense for the Christian—they are turned away

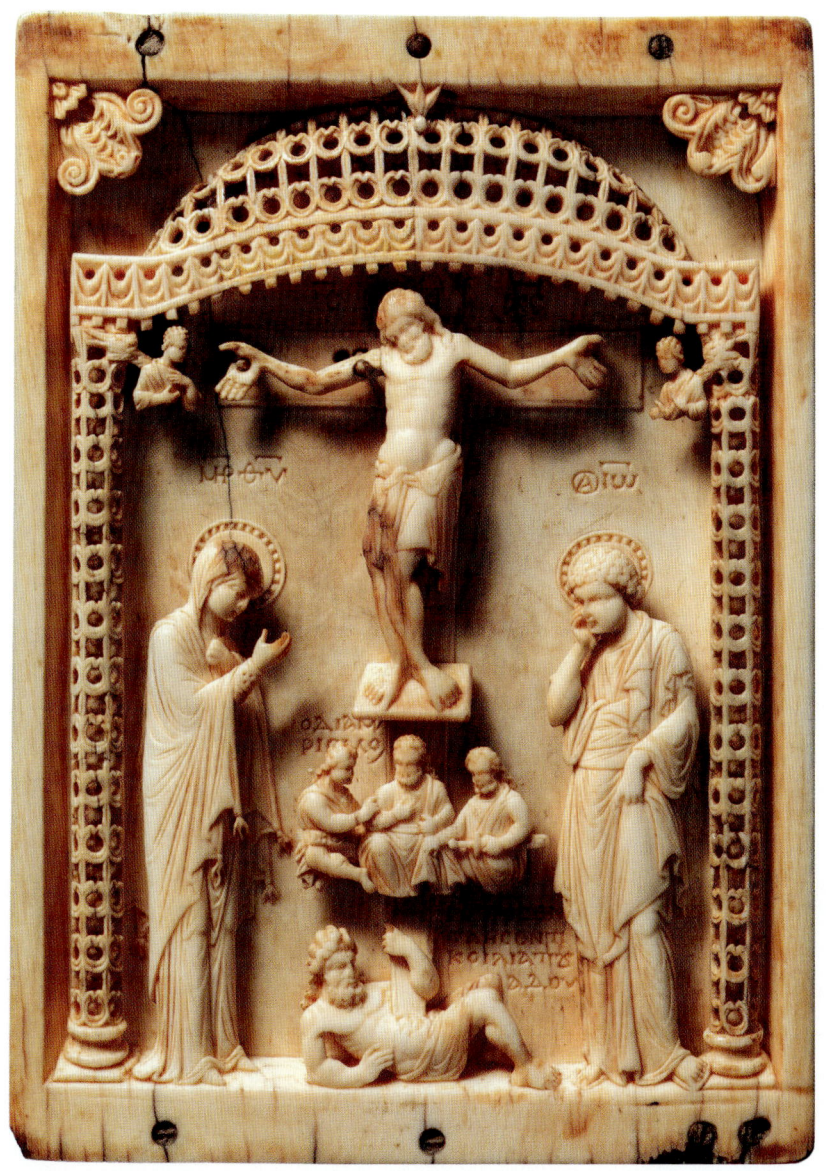

Figure 20. *Icon with the Crucifixion*, mid-10th century. Ivory, 15.1 × 8.9 × 0.8 cm. Metropolitan Museum of Art, New York. (Photo: Metropolitan Museum of Art)

from Christ and against Hades—that is, death (fig 20). The sixth-century Byzantine hymnist Romanos has Hades ask, "Who has fixed a nail in my heart?"; then he complains of a lance that is piercing and tearing him, causing agony. Romanos concludes the hymn by describing how Hades, because of the torture, relinquished the bodies of those in Hell. The evil body suffers and becomes a belly or mouth that disgorges the dead, while the body of Christ remains victorious over suffering. In this vividly somatic hymn, the Passion and its tortures literally saves souls. As Georgia Frank has argued, the later Byzantine ivory represents Hades pierced through the belly by the Cross under the crucified, but ultimately victorious figure of Christ.[10]

In a third variant, this one expressing their value as objects, even loot, the Passion instruments are (fictively) collected as trophies of victory. Such assemblages recall collections of enemy weapons depicted by Hellenistic and Roman artists, often with defeated soldiers slumped nearby (fig. 21). On an early Christian sarcophagus in the Vatican (fig. 22), the formula is used to evoke the soldiers guarding Christ's tomb, although they sit to either side of the Christogram, the Chi-Rho standard of Constantine that rises between them. On either side of this central image are narrative scenes from the Passion; to the left is one of the first depictions of the Crowning of Christ. Rather than thorns, however, Christ's crown is the same laurel wreath "of victory" as the one that encircles the Chi-Rho monogram at the center of the sarcophagus.[11]

Similarly, an early medieval manuscript, the Utrecht Psalter of circa 820, includes a depiction of the Passion instruments piled around the Cross in its illustration of Psalm 21 (fig. 23). The appearance of these instruments has been described as a response to the Psalter text understood to foretell the treatment of Christ's robe at the Crucifixion: "They parted my garments amongst them; and upon my vesture they cast lots." (Ps. 21:19). The contested garment is pictured independently in the miniature, but it may have

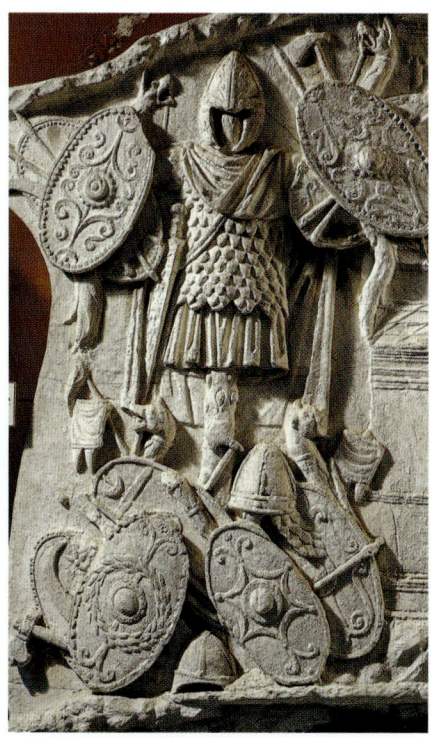

Figure 21. *Five Good Emperors* (detail of trophies of Dacian weapons), 113 CE. Plaster cast from Trajan's Column, National Historical Museum, Bucharest. (Photo: © DEA / G. Dagli Orti / De Agostini / Getty Images)

suggested the topic of Passion instruments to the artist. In a separate vignette, above and to the right, the Cross is shown as a central standard upon which they are draped as signs of victory: the lance, the sponge on a lance, the whip, and the crown as a laurel wreath. This victorious representation of the Cross may be understood to be inspired by later verses of the psalm: "For the kingdom is the Lord's; and he shall have dominion over the nations" (Ps. 21:29) and "The heavens shall shew forth his justice" (Ps. 21:32). Such assertions of triumph, as we have seen in the previous chapter, began with Constantine's imperial use of the cross but were remarkably persistent

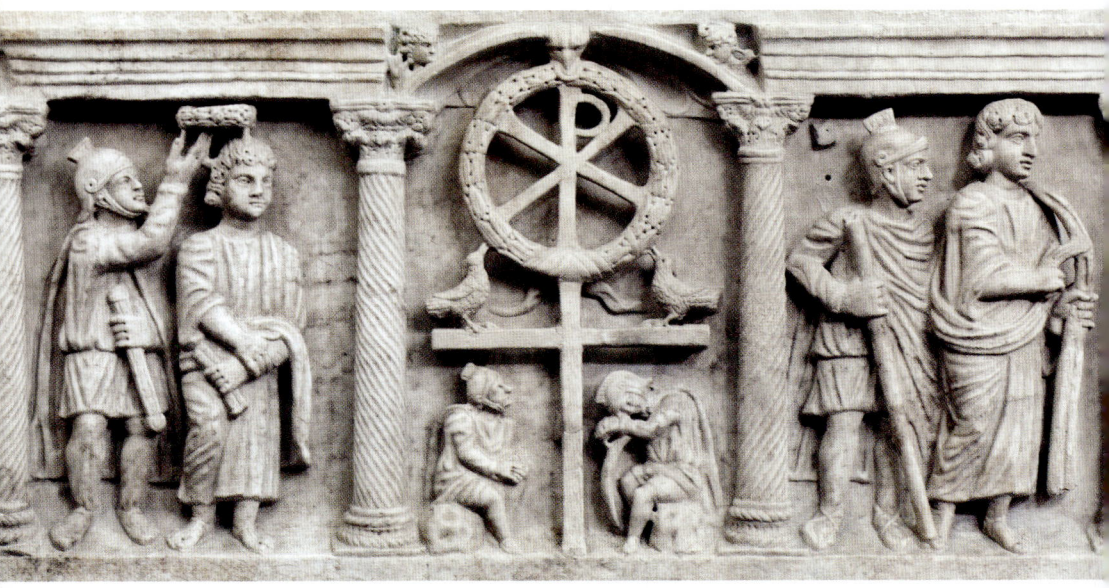

Figure 22. *Passion Sarcophagus* (detail), c. 350 CE. Marble, 59 × 202 × 80 cm. Vatican Museums, Vatican City. (Photo: © Genevra Kornbluth)

throughout the Middle Ages. They culminated in the late Middle Ages in the paradox of the *Arma Christi*—the weapons that both tortured Christ and allowed him to triumph.

In this sort of triumphal imagery, victory is elided with power, and the authority to rule and to judge is secured by means of the collection of weapons, a truism evident not only in Roman imagery but also in Biblical prophecy. In the Gospel of Matthew (24:30), the "sign of the Son of Man" (that is, the cross) was to appear in the heavens at the moment of Judgment. During the eleventh and twelfth centuries, the Passion instruments continued to be associated with the prophecy from Matthew and were clustered around the cross in images of the Last Judgment.[12] Hence, the instruments are clearly depicted as, in effect, weaponized, held by the angels who stand guard at

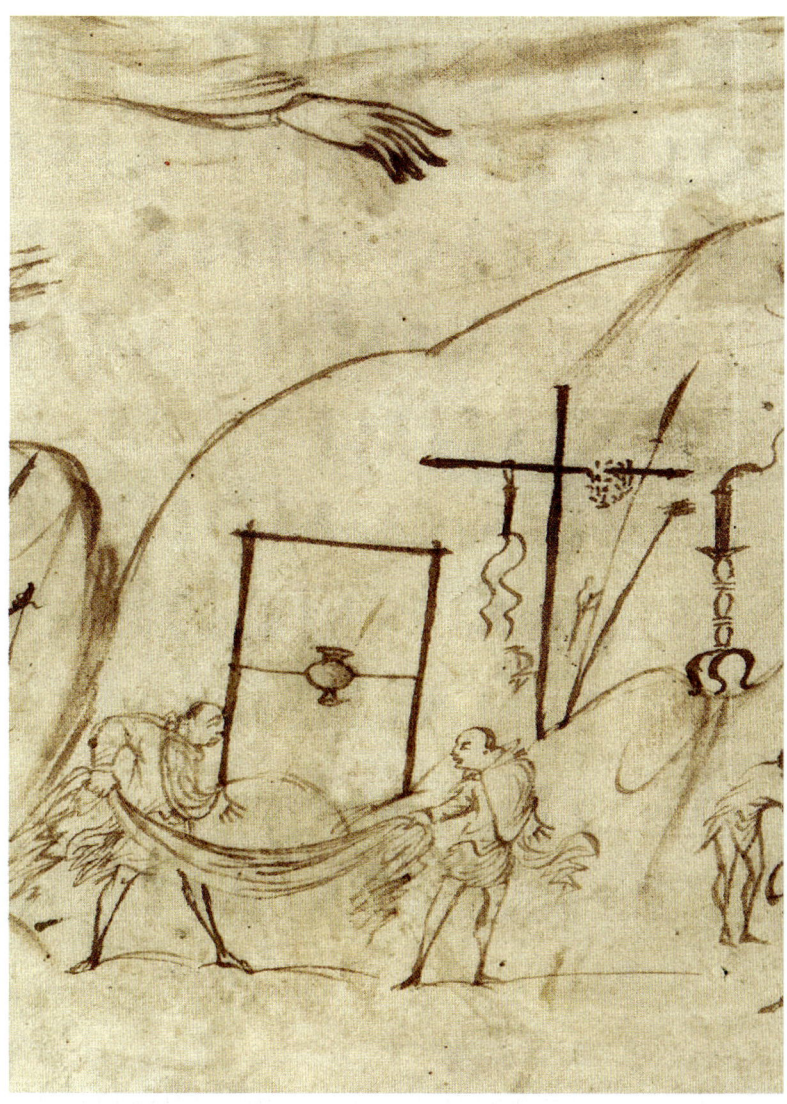

Figure 23. Detail of illustration for Psalm 21/22, *Utrecht Psalter*, Hs. 32, fol. 12r, c. 820–35. Manuscript, 33 × 25.5 cm. Utrecht University Library. (Photo: © Utrecht University Library)

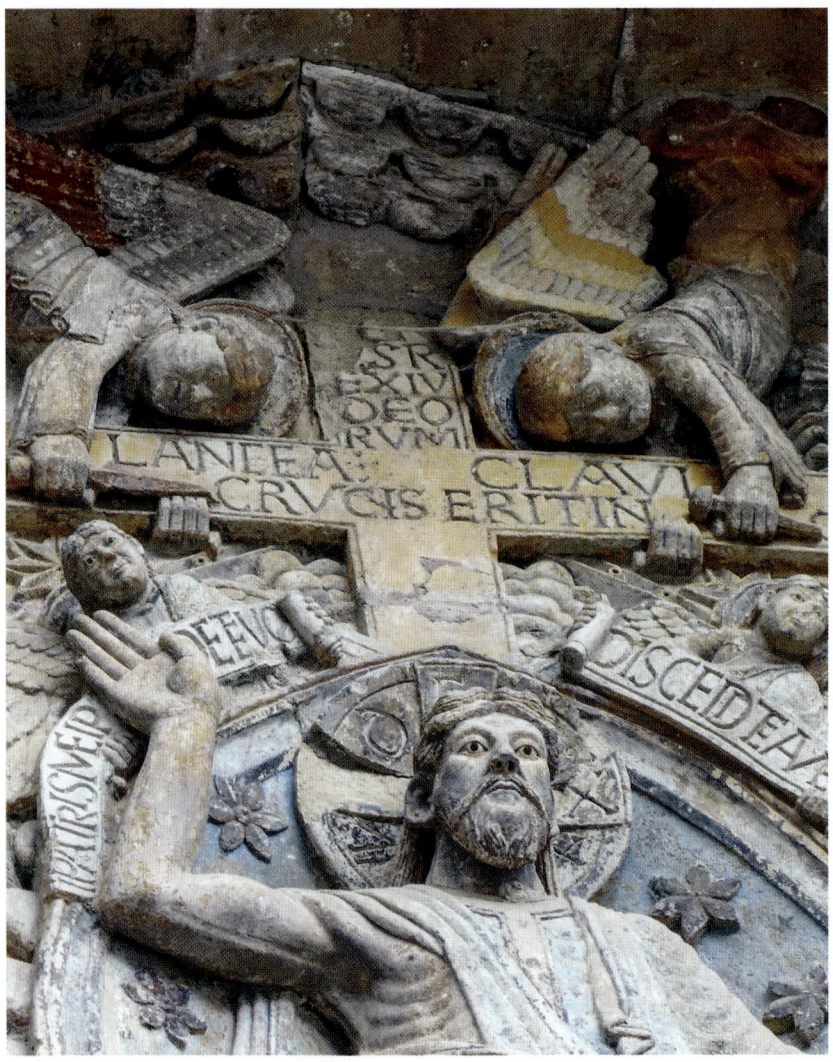

Figure 24. *Tympanum of Sainte-Foi* (detail), early 12th century. Painted limestone relief. Church of Sainte-Foi, Conques, France. (Photo: © Cynthia Hahn)

either side of the Enthroned Christ (see fig. 24). On the Klosterneuberg Altar, made in 1181, Nicholas of Verdun surrounds his image of the Judging Christ with an inscription that makes the connection between suffering and empowerment explicit: "Those for whom I have suffered shall see me, whose judge I now am."[13] In some cases, such representations of Passion relics are for the first time associated with material relics. The church of Sainte-Foi at Conques had Passion relics in its treasury, and its sculpted portal depicts angels presenting the lance, the nails, and the Cross as Christ raises his right arm in judgment (fig. 24).[14]

## PASSION RELICS AS THINGS

As we turn from texts and images to a consideration of surviving material relics, the task we have set ourselves is daunting. Although we are concerned with relics certified by faith rather than by other means of authentication, still the situation is murky. Fortunately, for the purposes of this investigation, we will find that art serves as clarification in many ways. Indeed, the evidence of art works and reliquaries will prove essential to our task, not only for resolving questions of identification but also for charting a terrain, which in some sense concerns the social history of the imagination. We will see that the great collections of Passion relics were consistently publicized and magnified with gorgeous architectural surrounds and spectacularly beautiful reliquaries, whose ultimate purpose was to explain the importance and meaning of the relics. Furthermore, representation in art parallels or even precedes many developments in the cults of Passion relics. For example, it is only with the emergence of the Crown of Thorns as a preeminent Crusade relic that it becomes ubiquitous in representations of the Crucifixion and that the thorns begin to prick and draw blood in images of the Passion. Similarly, the artistic conventions governing the depiction of the Crucifixion (whether Christ's feet are separated or overlapped) controlled the preferred number of Holy Nails—that is, three or four.[15] Finally, as we have already seen, the cross can be rendered as a wooden one or as a metal liturgical cross in any given pictorial representation, reflecting its importance for use in ceremony and prayer.

Indeed, imagination and the stubbornly physical object work in synergy in relic veneration.[16] Shining reliquaries present bits of wood, iron, and plant matter or cloth as immeasurably precious things; inscription, text, and well-trained religious sensibilities initiate a story about them. Ultimately, the physical object provides an unparalleled and indispensable focus for meditation and prayer, and art magnifies and focuses the effect.

But, unfortunately, not all relics have sanctioned stories and provenances that reconstruct their history and reassure the faithful that they are genuine. Although, ultimately, faith trumps more precise evidence, during the modern "scientific age" of the last few centuries, much energy has been invested in tracing unbroken provenances of various relics, even when the documented record has many gaps.[17] Such historical documentation will not be our concern in the main, but it deserves a modicum of attention. A list of the primary relics and their circumstances and materials will help orient the reader to the relics and their histories or the lack thereof (the Crown of Thorns is omitted from this list and is discussed separately).

As we have already seen, the most precisely documented relic is the True Cross, said to have been found by Empress Helena some three hundred years after the Crucifixion in a pit at the site of Golgotha near where Christ was purported to be buried. The True Cross is often said to have been found along with the nails and the *titulus* (the board generally marked with the letters INRI in Crucifixion images), although there are competing textual traditions.[18] There are no widely accepted legends concerning the discovery of the other major implements, such as the Crown of Thorns, the lance, or any of the various holy cloths.

*Holy Nails*

After the relic of the True Cross, the nails are the most prominent of the early relics. Variously numbered at two, three, or four,[19] they were said to have been found by Helena in a second moment after the discovery of the True Cross and the crosses of the thieves with whom Christ was crucified, although alternative accounts exist. Indeed, once again (as with the Cross and the "Dream of the Rood"), an Anglo-Saxon poet captures the essence of the relics and their story. In Cynewulf's *Elene*, when the empress is excavating the Cross, rather than experience the tribulations of an archaeologist and struggle to differentiate rusted iron from clots of earth, Helena spots the nails immediately. In what is something of an alchemical miracle, the nails gleam like gold in the soil. However, rather than insist upon a change of the essential material of these relics, this miracle emphasizes the more general light-emitting quality of relics.[20]

Indeed, the iron of the nails is an essential part of their nature. Although blunt, hard, and elemental, (unalloyed) iron is a noble material mentioned in the Bible: it was among those Solomon used to build the Temple, and it was fully worthy of being kept in a treasury (1 Chron. 29:2, Josh. 6:19). It is also distinguished as being an almost magical material of infinite malleability. Remarkably, the potency of the material can be enhanced through its use for execution, as pre-Christian sources testify.[21] Indeed, iron and other materials associated with sudden death were amuletic,[22] and in pre-Christian and non-Christian cultures alike, iron was thought to protect against the evil eye.[23]

In one of those reversals so typical of relic devotion, the heavy iron of the nails is praised as infinitely attractive by Thiofrid of Echternach (d. 1110) in the only medieval treatise on relics: "Oh how holy, how precious, how sweet, how lovable and delectable is the iron material of these nails."[24] The devotee praying the thirteenth-century *Stimulus amoris* asks the nails to "fix my hands and feet to [the cross]."[25] In the later Middle Ages, Margery Kempe singles out the nail among the Passion instruments, calling it "boisterous," testifying to its lively ability to surpass its lumpen materiality.[26]

According to legend, Helena's first act upon the discovery of the nails was to divide them: one or possibly two were delivered to her son, who had them forged into a helmet and a bridle.[27] This action is not only that of a virtuous smithy, but it also fulfills the Old Testament prophecy "In that day shall there be upon the bells of the horses, Holiness unto the Lord" (Zech. 14:20). In the Christian tradition, especially the writing of Ambrose, the object becomes a bridle for the horse—that is, a restraint, whereas the helmet with the nail at the emperor's forehead means that this holy material "rules" the empire.

Changeability or malleability is not only a legendary aspect of the nails—a number of the remaining relics of the nails survive because they are part of other relic objects. One is said to be part of the Holy Lance in Vienna (discussed below). Another is secreted in the interior of the "iron crown of Italy" at Monza (see fig. 19, top), a relic crown purported to be fashioned with the nail from Constantine's helm.[28] The latter relic, although renowned as the crown used for the coronation of the king of Italy and even called upon for the coronation of Napoleon in 1805,[29] seems not to be early Christian but instead is dated to the Carolingian era.

A nail relic at Trier is noteworthy for its integrity and may be the one that Thiofrid of Echternach praised (fig. 25). It is enclosed in a reliquary that precisely follows its shape and uniquely emphasizes the wholeness and large size of the surviving relic. It is easily removed from its container and is customarily displayed without its reliquary today.[30] There are also whole nails venerated at Santa Croce in Gerusalemme in Rome and in the cathedral treasury in Essen, Germany (originally from the women's monastery there). The Holy Nail in the Sienese hospital of Santa Maria della Scala was obtained from Constantinople,[31] and a nail claimed to be the one donated by Charles

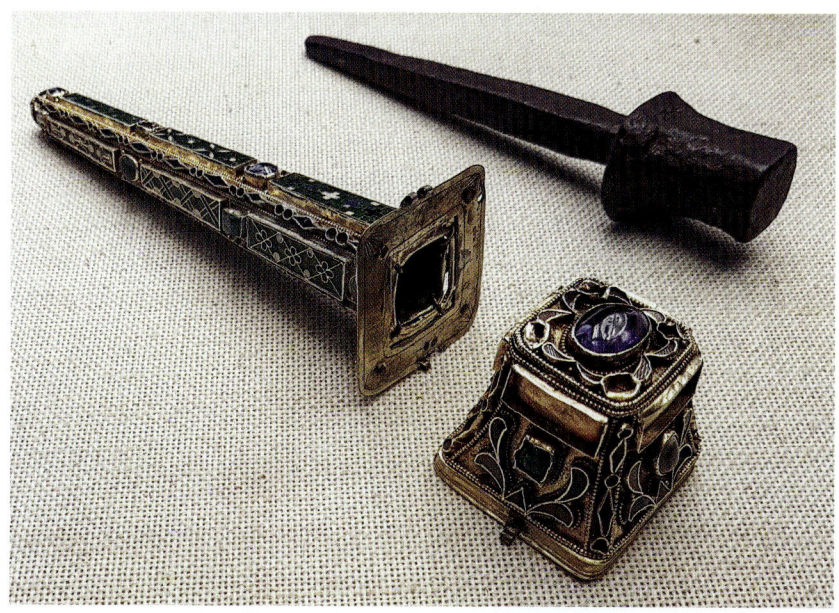

Figure 25. *Reliquary of the Holy Nail*, 9th–10th century. Gold, cloisonné enamel, precious stones, 21.4 cm (length). Cathedral Treasury, Trier. (Photo: © Kelon3 / Wikimedia Commons / CC BY-SA 4.0)

the Bald (or also said to be given by Charlemagne) was displayed at Saint-Denis before the French revolution. One author lists twenty-nine cities that claim to possess nail relics.[32]

One final and essential quality of the nail is its metaphorical ability to "fix," or fasten. Obviously, it was the instrument that penetrated Christ's hands and feet, brutally pinning his body to the cross. In devotional texts about the nail, we will see that it functions as the element that bluntly strikes and fixes the mind, particularly in the memory system that makes up the *Arma Christi*. It also is said to join together earth and heaven.[33]

## The Titulus

The *titulus* is a somewhat more obscure relic. Saint John Chrysostom and Ambrose both claim that it was still attached to the Cross when Helena discovered it—it was said to help her distinguish the True Cross from the crosses of the thieves.[34] Among the primary Passion relics, it is distinctive for being one of the few that are not instruments of torture. However, like Christ's purple cloak, in naming Christ King of the Jews, it is intended as an object of humiliation, but ultimately it is capable of turning the tables on mockery by announcing the truth of Christ's kingship. Many depictions of the *titulus* show only the four letters INRI, an abbreviation for Jesus Nazarenus, Rex Iudorum (Jesus of Nazareth, King of the Jews). But the Gospel of John (19:19–20) specifies that the title spelled out the inscription in three languages: Greek, Latin, and Hebrew, making it, in Biblical terms, an inscription that should have been legible to everyone and any audience. The relic in Santa Croce in Gerusalemme in Rome (fig. 26), putatively deposited by Helena herself, has attracted attention due to its multilingual nature, although the authenticity of the inscription has certainly also been greeted with skepticism.[35] A few medieval representations of the trilingual *titulus* survive, but none seem related to the relic.[36]

## The Lance

The importance of the lance as a relic predates that of the *titulus*, but no clear provenance survives for it. Indeed, the lance is one case in which the multiplication of relics is problematic. There should just be one relic of the lance; it is neither as potentially divisible as the wood of the Cross and *titulus* (although various explanations describe a tip broken off), nor is it naturally numerous or forged into other objects like the nails (although there are exceptions—according to the *Chanson de Roland*, Charlemagne's sword held a relic of the lance).[37] Nevertheless, a number of lances survive even today, each of which is claimed to be the unique, historical weapon used at the

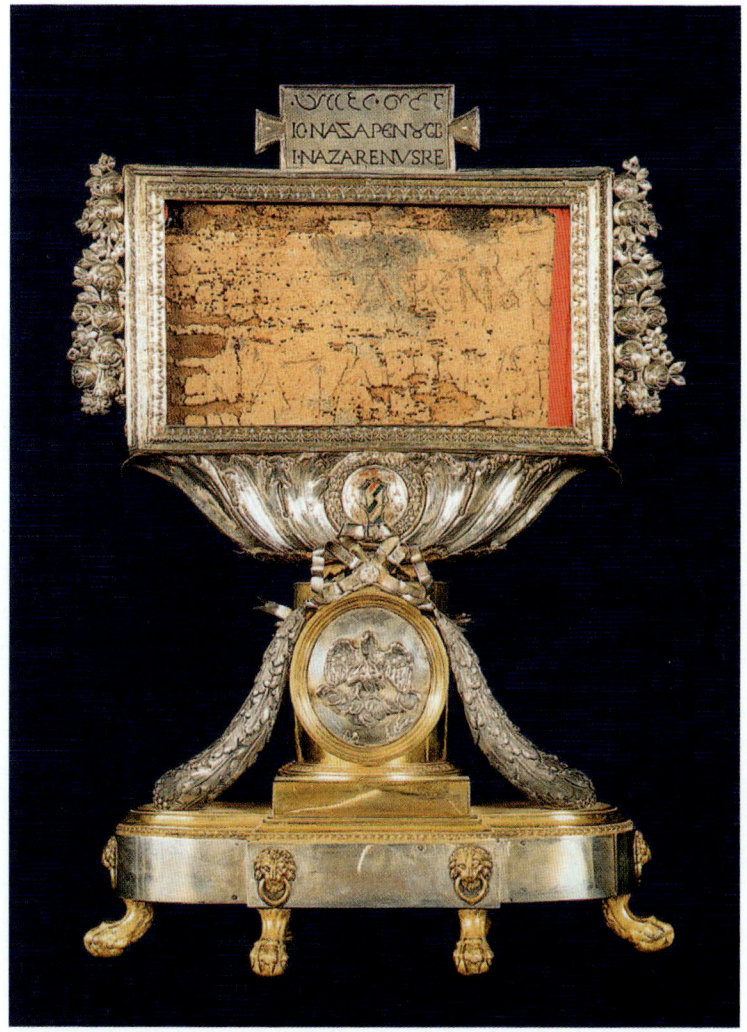

Figure 26. *Titulus Crucis*. Walnut panel, 25.3 × 14 cm; silver reliquary frame, early 16th century. Santa Croce in Gerusalemme, Rome. (Photo: Primeros cristianos, www.primeroscristianos.com)

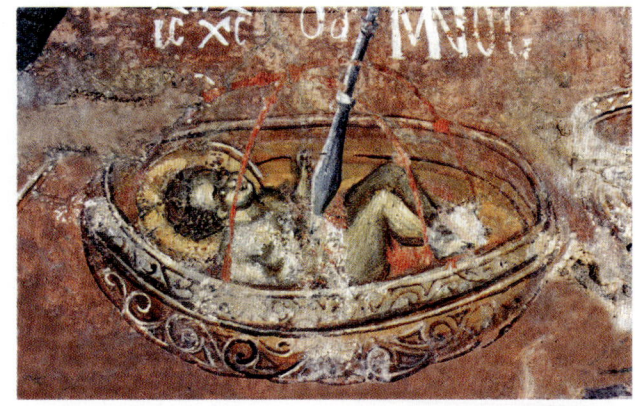

Figure 27. *The Melismos*, second quarter of 14th century. Wall fresco. Church of St. John the Baptist, Axos, Mylopotamos, Crete. (Photo: © Ioannis Spatharakis, Alexandros Press)

Crucifixion to pierce Christ's side. As the implement of the deathblow, the lance created the wound that is thought of as the foundation of the Church, the source of the water and the blood that emerged from Christ's side signifying the baptism and the Eucharist. In the Orthodox liturgy, the import of that blow is commemorated when the priest pierces the Host with a liturgical spear before its division in honor of the Trinity. The imagery of Middle Byzantine frescoes makes the action all the more vivid as the Host is depicted as the Christ Child suffering from the attack (fig. 27).[38]

The Gospel of John does not identify the soldier who wielded the lance, but a name for him, Longinus, occurs already in fourth-century apocryphal Gospels. By the sixth and seventh centuries, the presence of the lance is attested in Jerusalem, in some sources at the Church of Sion, in others at the Holy Sepulcher.[39] The Jerusalem lance was taken to Constantinople, and perhaps the tip was acquired by Louis IX, the king of France, for the Sainte-Chapelle, although that relic does not survive. Another fragment of the lance was presented to Pope Innocent VIII in 1492 by Sultan Bajazet, the son of Mohomet II, and it was eventually embedded along with three other significant relics into the piers of St. Peter's Basilica in Rome.

The lance with the most storied history, now in Vienna (fig. 28),[40] is the oldest part of the regalia of the Holy Roman Empire that resided for a long time in the city of Nuremberg. Used since 1273 as part of the imperial coronation ceremony, it is also known as the lance of Maurice, the famous soldier-saint and patron of the German empire, and eventually acquired the rather histrionic name the Spear of Destiny. It may actually be a Carolingian lance, but that original object has additions dating from the same era in iron, silver, and gold. The iron is said to be a portion of one of the nails. The mix of metals is noted in particular by Thiofrid, who called attention to the special quality of its materials, pronouncing that it contains "every metal" and calling it "salutaris lanceae," the lance of salvation.[41]

There are competing lances in Vagharshapat (previously known as Echmiadzin), the religious capital of Armenia, attested since the thirteenth century, and in Kraków, Poland, also known from the thirteenth century. The Germans claim the Polish example is a copy that incorporates a small sliver of the original, and they say the same of a "copy" in Hungary. A lance relic in England that in the twelfth century William of Malmesbury claimed was given to Aethelstan by the German emperor has not survived.

One significant and long-standing characteristic of these lances is their association with royal and imperial owners. Indeed, the Viennese lance acquired the name the Spear of Destiny because it was thought to be instrumental in the rise and fall of the Third Reich. The Vienna relic was hidden during World War II in a vault in Nuremburg along with the other imperial regalia.[42] In the Middle Ages, the lance was in Nuremburg along with other imperial relics, where an office was written and a devotion developed that celebrated the wounds of Christ and eventually focused on a wound in the heart.[43] Furthermore, perhaps a sort of contact relic multiplication was established in which the relic was used to pierce vellum, a material that, in the context of sacred books, was often compared to Christ's skin.[44]

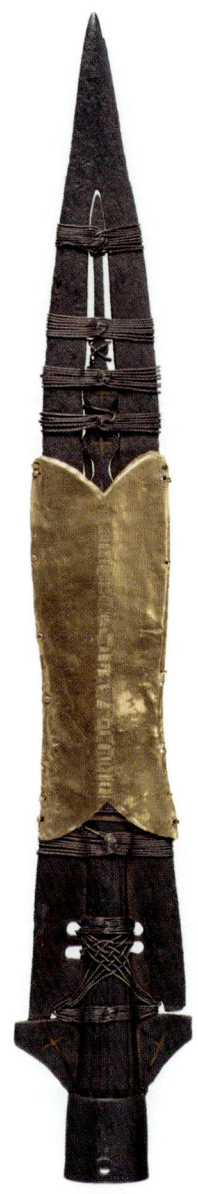

Figure 28. *The Holy Lance,* 8th century (silver cuff: second half of 11th century; gold cuff: third quarter of 14th century). Steel, iron, brass, silver, gold, and leather, 50.7 cm (length). Kunsthistorisches Museum, Vienna. (Photo: © KHM-Museumsverband)

Finally, of course, we should recall the remarkable story, told in chapter 1, of the discovery of a lance in Antioch during the Crusaders' siege (1097-98). An illustration in *Passages d'outremer* by Sébastien Mamerot circa 1474 shows its discovery inside a church whose sculptures attached to the interior columns recall the Sainte-Chapelle (fig. 29). With the Apostles overseeing the procedure, the finding of the lance is put in its proper context—that of a Holy Land relic of rare importance. Of course, its story took a turn for the worse (see chapter 1), and that relic was also lost.

*Cloth Relics, the Sponge, the Column*
The various cloth relics—the seamless robe, the purple robe, the shroud and burial cloths, even the Veronica (the famous relic of the miraculous imprint of Christ's face)—were not important relics (except in Byzantium) until the later Middle Ages. Relic inventories mention diverse cloths, but for the most part it is only with the rise of the importance of the Veronica in Rome and the Turin Shroud at the Savoy court that cloths become widely renowned relics—that is, more than a small part of larger collections. These relics will be discussed more fully below.

In its early renown, the seamless robe (John 19:23-24) is something of an exception among textile relics. It is attested as a relic in as many as thirty different treasuries. Many of these examples must be fragments although the most venerated relic, at Trier, is purported to be whole and to be the gift of Helena (along with the Trier nail, mentioned above; see fig. 25).[45] The earliest documentation to the empress's gift of the robe occurs in the vita of Saint Agritius, the fourth-century bishop of Trier. That text is dated to the eleventh century, and the relic notably was "found" in the cathedral in 1196. The actual object may possibly be identified as Byzantine fabric of the fifth or sixth century.[46] It still is the focus of pilgrimage today (fig. 30).[47]

The sponge is also a late arrival as an object with status as an independent relic. It is mentioned in the Gospels by Mark (15:36), Matthew (27:48), and

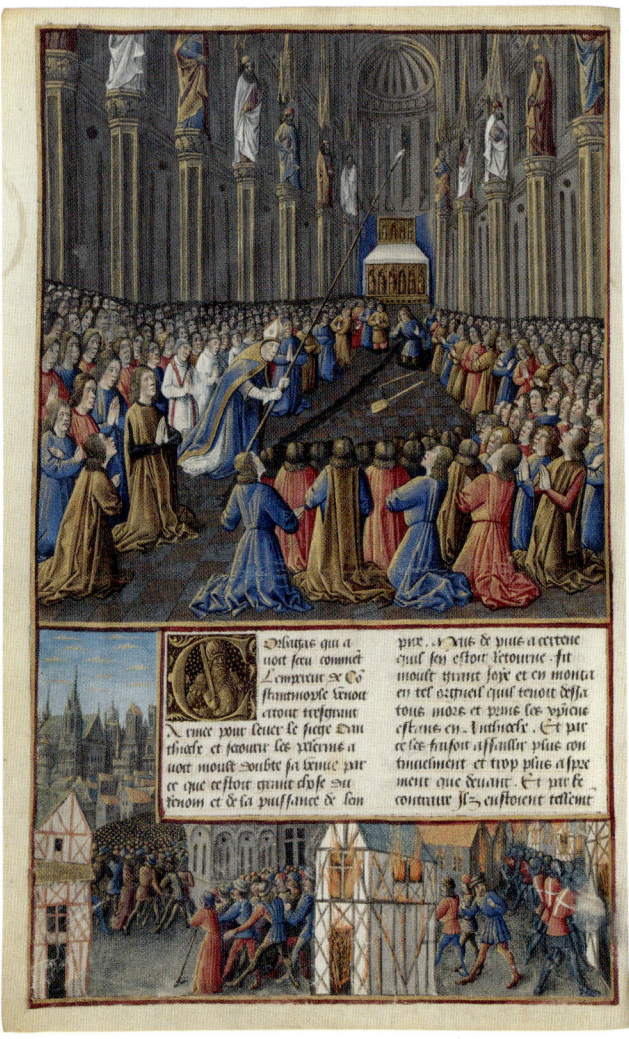

Figure 29. "Invention of the Holy Lance in Jerusalem" (top), in Sébastien Mamerot, *Passages d'outremer,* MS Fr. 5594, fol. 67v, c. 1474. Vellum manuscript. Bibliothèque nationale de France, Paris. (Photo: © Bibliothèque nationale de France)

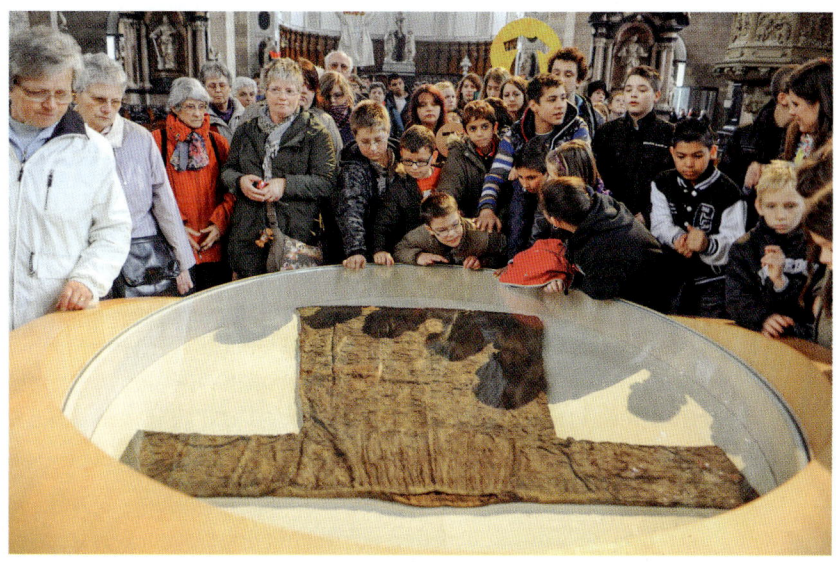

Figure 30. *Holy Robe in Trier*. Trier Cathedral, Trier. (Photo: Wikimedia Commons)

John (19:29), but first mentioned as materially present in Jerusalem only in the sixth century by Gregory of Tours. Its presence there is subsequently confirmed in the seventh century by Sophronius of Jerusalem, who notes that it is located in the Jerusalem Martyrium. Patrikios Niketas, the son of Shahrbaraz (from whom Heraclius won back the captured relic of the True Cross), sent a relic of the sponge to Constantinople, so a relic must have remained in Jerusalem while the city was under the control of the Persians.[48] The recovered relic was attached to the True Cross and displayed in Hagia Sophia for veneration on 14 September 629. The lance arrived shortly thereafter, and that relic was venerated for four full days in the Byzantine capital.

Many of the images that show angels holding the two "weapons" reflect a ceremonial pairing of the lance and sponge. The *Triptych Reliquary of the True*

*Cross* (see fig. 6) depicts such angels on either side of a True Cross relic, which stands in for Christ, but in the pediment above, a wreath-like Crown of Thorns is paired with the bowl of vinegar to the right and left of the judging Christ in heaven to represent the rewards of the blessed and the punishments of the damned.

The sponge seems to have remained in Constantinople until well after the Sack of 1204, and it was transferred to Paris with the other Passion relics that King Louis IX acquired in 1239. Its whereabouts now is uncertain, but Rome claims to have at least two relics, one at the Lateran and one at Santa Croce in Gerusalemme. The sponge has the advantage of being an indefinitely shaped material that could be readily divided and shared as a relic, and, as we will see, a portion of it was said to have been given to the fourteenth-century Holy Roman emperor Charles IV for Prague.

The column to which Christ was tied during his flagellation was important already in the early pilgrimage era because it served as a focus of devotion in Jerusalem. Visiting the relic involved a performative veneration for pilgrims, who wrote of touching it and observing the marks on its surface.[49] It began to appear among Passion relics in depictions during the twelfth century,[50] and fragments of the relic were widely shared and became part of many relic collections.

*Holy Blood*
Christ's blood can be considered a Passion relic, but it has a history too complex and contested to attempt to explore more than superficially here. Theologians argued that no blood of Christ survived from the time of the Crucifixion and that blood relics were produced only through miracles and the Eucharist. In romance and legend, the Holy Grail was claimed not only to be the container (in effect, a reliquary) of the original blood of the Eucharist of the Last Supper but also to have been used by Joseph of Arimathea to collect

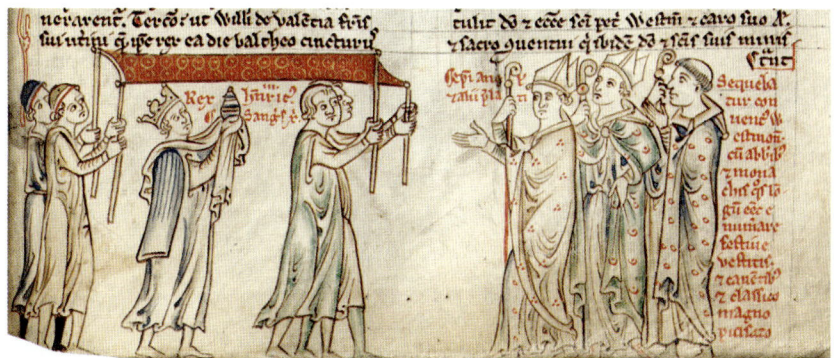

Figure 31. "Translation of the Holy Blood," in Matthew Paris, *Chronica Maiora II*, CCCC MS 16, fol. 216r, 13th century. Vellum manuscript, 35.8 × 24.4 cm. Parker Library, Corpus Christi College, Cambridge. (Photo: © Parker Library, Corpus Christi College)

blood at the Crucifixion. In something of a parallel to the ascended body of Christ, however, "the Grail is finally withdrawn by divine agency into heaven," never to be seen on earth again.[51] Despite these theological arguments and notable legendary disappearance, numerous blood relics were the center of devotional cults. Furthermore, miraculous Host relics marked with blood proliferated throughout late medieval Europe.[52]

Indeed, blood relics came to have marked political importance. The king of England Henry III received a relic of the Holy Blood and a letter attesting to its authenticity from the Patriarch of Jerusalem, and he celebrated its *adventus* to England in 1247. As Matthew Paris noted in his chronicle, the ceremony was very similar to those with which Louis had celebrated the reception of the Crown of Thorns and the True Cross: Henry walked barefoot, carried the relic himself, and kept his eyes fixed on his treasure, perhaps in hopes that the relic would serve as England's powerful holy token as the Crown had for France (fig. 31).[53] Other celebrated blood relics appear

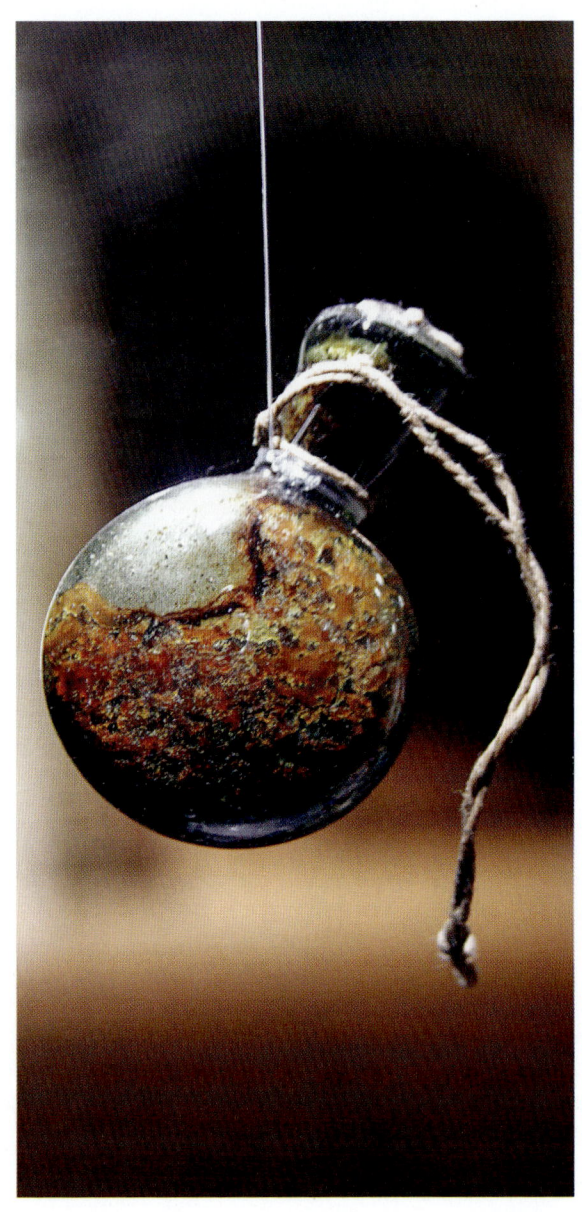

Figure 32. *Reliquary of the Blood of Christ* ("Beirut ampulla"), 8th century. Santa Maria Della Scala, Siena. (Photo: © José Luiz Bernardes Ribeiro / Wikimedia Commons / CC BY-SA 4.0)

in Sant'Andrea in Mantua (purportedly earth scooped up by Longinus, rediscovered circa 1049),[54] in Bruges, and at Weingarten Abbey in Germany (a portion of the Mantua relic), as well as numerous other locations.

The Holy Blood relic in Bruges arrived in 1150 in the form of a cloth or bit of earth saturated with blood, as the gift of the Crusader Thierry, Count of Flanders, a participant in the second Crusade (a donor still commemorated today in processions). The relic became the center of important civic rituals of independence from French "tyranny" and gave rise to devotions in the fifteenth century and later in which the "fountain of life" granted grace via blood.[55]

Numerous so-called Beirut ampullae (fig. 32) disseminated across Europe contain blood miraculously emitted from an icon as recounted in an anti-Semitic story circulated from as early as the ninth century in the East. The relic was credited with a powerful ability to heal and convert.[56] Imaginative devotions to blood were influential.[57]

## PASSION RELICS COLLECTED

Notwithstanding some of the fascinating legends and rapturous devotions centered on singular objects, our discussion of Passion relics cannot linger on individual relics but must turn in a decidedly different direction. Rather than attempt to confirm the existence of true relics, an authenticity put into doubt not only by the late reports of the discovery of most of the relics but also most certainly by multiple and competitive claimants to legitimacy, we can more profitably turn our attention to the way these objects were used, perceived, and displayed. The most striking, but little recognized aspect of Passion relics is that they so often appear in groups.

Even if individual relic fragments had little or no guarantee of authenticity, in powerful groupings Passion relics won their owners very real religious and political prestige. A summary history of such collections will reveal that it was their status as ensembles, as part of larger collections, and, therefore, their nature in projecting greater strength together that inspired emperors and prelates to seek them out and spend fortunes to obtain them.

The first great relic collections of renown were those in Jerusalem and Constantinople, the preeminent Christian capitals. The collections in Jerusalem were undoubtedly the culmination of various acts of identification of local substances and objects in individual moments of *inventio* (discovery) native to a pilgrimage community in a pervasively holy environment (many undoubtedly were the product of wishful thinking or overeager devotees). In Jerusalem, both the Holy Sepulcher and the Sion basilica had significant collections of relic objects. The Holy Sepulcher, of course, had the tomb, but it also had the Stone of Unction, and the Cross, reed, sponge, and lance. Sion had the column, the Crown of Thorns, the lance, and reed.[58] In contrast to such native riches and more happenstance assemblages, Constantinople's treasuries represent purposefully assembled collections, the result of acts of sometimes forceful importation of holy matter with the express purpose of sanctifying the city and the Byzantine Empire.

The Eastern capital had a significant relic of the Cross, as well as other Passion relics at least from the time of Heraclius, but in the tenth and eleventh centuries a more definitive collection of such relics seems to have come together in the Pharos, the palace chapel. Because the Byzantine emperors could obtain almost any desired relic through a sort of religious eminent domain, many relics came to the Eastern capital in well-recorded ceremonies of *adventus*. Others—for example, the Crown of Thorns—seem to have arrived with nary a mention in the historical record. The collections in both Hagia Sophia and the Pharos chapel were visited by many pilgrims and renowned throughout the Christian world. The Pharos collection included not only the Crown, a nail, the purple robe, and the reed but also the shackles of Satan and the towel from the foot washing before the Last Supper.[59]

In a decisive new stage of relic dissemination, due to the perfidious actions of the Crusaders of the Fourth Crusade in 1204, Constantinople became the unwilling bulk supplier of relics for transfer to collections in Europe. However, even before the Sack, the Eastern city was already a source of a purposefully controlled and minimal "trickle" of relics destined for European treasuries. That is, the Byzantine emperors who claimed to possess the largest portion of the relic of the True Cross knew that their ownership of that relic was a source of power. In many instances, a fragment was requested or a relic was given as a diplomatic gift and received with joy and acclamation. Indeed, Holger Klein has characterized relics of the True Cross as the most desired of all diplomatic gifts, valued even over precious materials or treasures of consummate workmanship.[60] The ability of the Byzantine emperor to control the material relic of the Cross represented unequalled political power and conferred enormous spiritual prestige upon Byzantium. It may have also been one factor to spur the looting of 1204.

So from this point of view, the story of the Crusades can be told as a history of the acquisition of relics and the control of shrines by a relic-hungry Europe. Purportedly, the Crusaders sought to protect the materials and places of the Holy Land from the depredations of the infidels, but they themselves were responsible for the transfer of many of these very relics to Europe, as was the case of the True Cross relic transferred to Toulouse (see discussion in chapter 1).

Crusading knights and churchmen returning with relic tokens from the wars in the East were able to bring prestige and glory to their lineage and institutions, usually through donations to and association with foundations or cathedrals.[61] In a society of fixed hierarchical relationships, Crusade triumphs and a gift of relics could shift long-established patterns of power. At Troyes Cathedral, stained-glass windows of the first quarter of the thirteenth century depict a monumental and highly visible commemoration of a gift of this sort. The imposing windows show a procession of clerics carrying relics obtained by Bishop Garnier de Traînel in Constantinople in the great giveaway of the relics of the sacked capital.[62]

In employing such strategies of enhancing political power and religious prestige through relics, the Crusaders and European kings surely borrowed a page from the Byzantine playbook. They had, however, an additional role model that they preferred and even revered: Charlemagne, the great Western emperor of the early Middle Ages, was closer to their hearts and heritage. According to the twelfth-century versified romance *Le Pèlerinage de Charlemagne*, although he was offered gems and riches by the emperor of Constantinople, the Carolingian emperor preferred relics.[63] Once more it is a thirteenth-century stained-glass window—this one, at Chartres Cathedral—that represents Charlemagne donating what looks like a crown to the cathedral (fig. 33). More accurately, the image may represent a donation of two Passion relics—a thorn from the Crown of Thorns and a nail—relics that the emperor is purported to have received from the patriarch of Jerusalem, again as reported in the fanciful text of the *Pèlerinage*.[64]

## The Crown of Thorns and Its History

Just as we turned to a singular case study in the last chapter, here, too, a historical example of one eagerly collected and disseminated Passion relic will give us a richer picture of the meaning and utilization of relics and collections. The Crown of Thorns is perhaps the most important of the Passion relics after the True Cross.[65] As a potential "frame" for the other relics, as well as for the suffering head of Christ, it is the relic that encompasses the others and hyperstimulates the imagination; even today, it is featured in tattoos and in profane song lyrics, and inspires high-fashion jewelry (fig. 34).

The *Pèlerinage*, the widely read legend detailing Charlemagne's visits to Jerusalem and Constantinople, may be, as suggested above, the origin of the Crusaders' interest in the Crown of Thorns.[66] As a relic that seems to have held little importance in Byzantium before about 1200, during and after the First Crusade, it gradually became one of the most desirable relics. Crusaders returned from the Holy Land bringing collections of splinters of the True

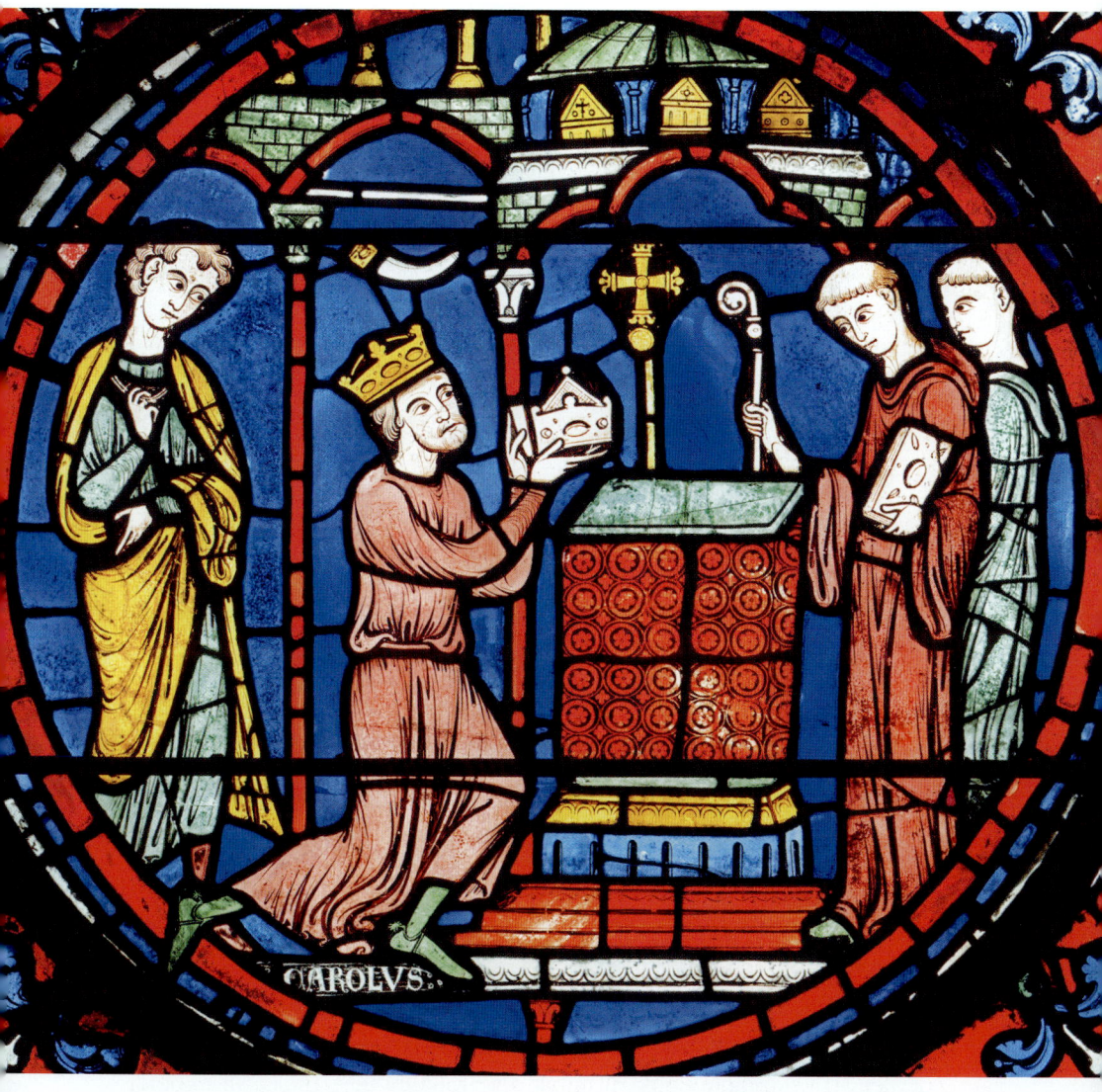

Figure 33. *Charlemagne Offers Relics to Chartres*, late 12th century. Stained glass, Chartres Cathedral, France. (Photo: © Alfredo Dagli Orti / Art Resource)

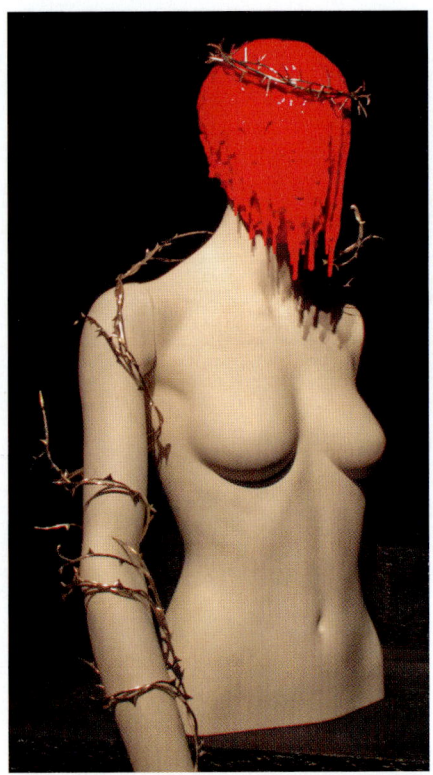

Figure 34. Shaun Leane (jeweler) for Alexander McQueen, *"Crown of Thorns" Headpiece and "Thorn" Armpiece*, Dante collection, fall-winter 1996–97. Silver. Headpiece at Metropolitan Museum, New York. (Photo: © Randy Duchaine / Alamy Stock Photo)

Cross and a host of other fragments, above all pebbles or stone relics evocative of holy sites. Once they added thorns to list of holy things to be obtained in the East, the desirability of the thorn relic soared.

One wonders just who realized how valuable it would be to acquire the relic of the Crown of Thorns in its entirety. Struggling to keep what was left of the Latin empire in Constantinople afloat, Baldwin II, the Latin emperor, found himself in dire need of funds. He wrote to his cousin King Louis IX for help. Was it Blanche of Castile, Louis's savvy and pious mother, who saw the opportunity? Or Bishop Cornut, who wrote the account of the reception of the Crown in France—and who was pictured with the Crown, again in stained glass, in a window from Tours Cathedral (fig. 35). Or perhaps, although busy preparing for another Crusade departure, it was Louis himself who saw the possibilities. Someone understood what the relic could do for France, and all three enthusiastically supported the process of acquiring it. In 1239, once the relic was redeemed from the Venetians, who had accepted it in pawn from Baldwin, plans were set in place to build an astonishing palace chapel that would house the incomparable relic—indeed a precious building with enormous stained-glass windows that has been called a reliquary "turned inside out" (fig. 36).[67]

No expense was spared in the construction of the Sainte-Chapelle, and it became one of the wonders of its age (or any age). Nonetheless, its cost, 40,000 gold livres, was dwarfed by the amount that was needed to redeem the relic: 135,000 livres. And let us remember this was not "buying" relics but rescuing them as a favor for Baldwin, a Crusader-king and relative, as Bishop Cornut took pains to explain. What did the Capetian king get for his investment? The Crown was not just any Passion relic, but one that was claimed to be miraculous through Christ's blood "always green" and even flowering. Furthermore, and even more important, King Louis, soon to be Saint Louis, was the conservator of not just a fragment of one of the Passion relics. He had the whole thing, no matter how many thorns were removed; the complete circle of the Crown attested that the French king had the privilege of ownership, which allowed him the exclusive right to dispense relics. Like the Byzantine emperors and their control of the True Cross relics, the French king could now be the source of much-desired gifts. I would argue that this is why the iconography of the crown insisted on representing the complete circle (see fig. 35), while at the same time Louis made much of giving away the individual thorns.

He did so with great ceremony and pomp.[68] If possible, the treasure of each thorn was conveyed by a trusted and spiritually superior messenger,

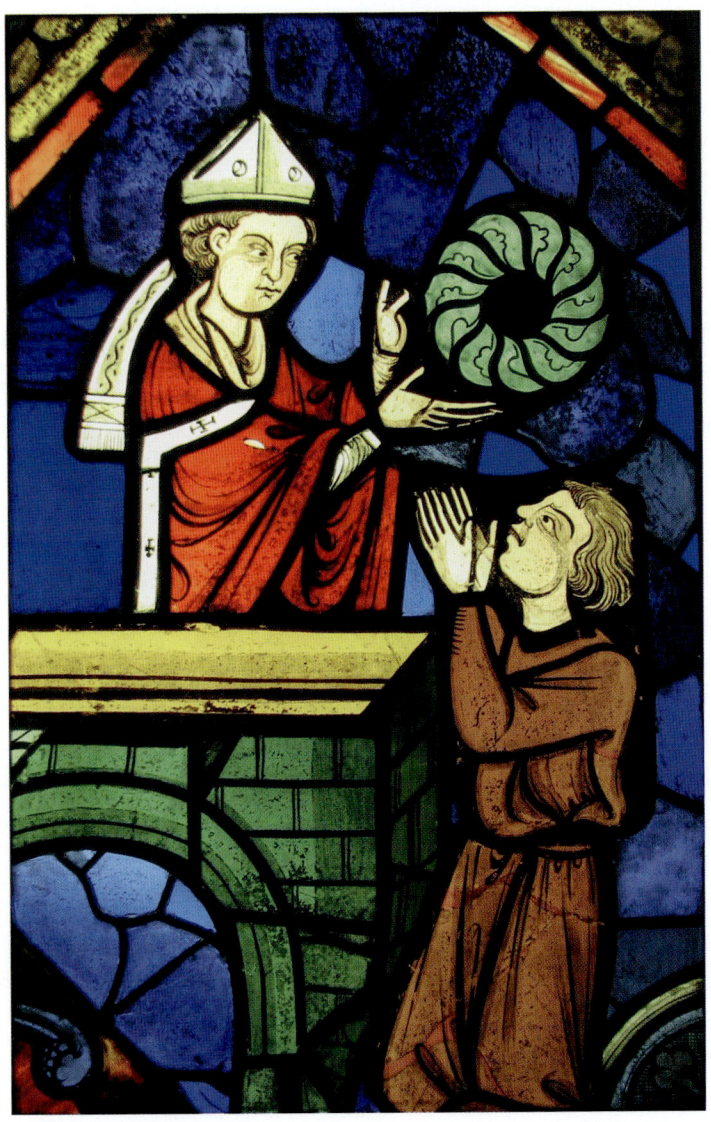

Figure 35. *Archbishop Gauthier Cornut of Sens Displaying the Crown of Thorns*, c. 1245–48. Stained glass panel, 55.2 × 34.9 cm. Metropolitan Museum of Art, New York. (Photo: Metropolitan Museum of Art)

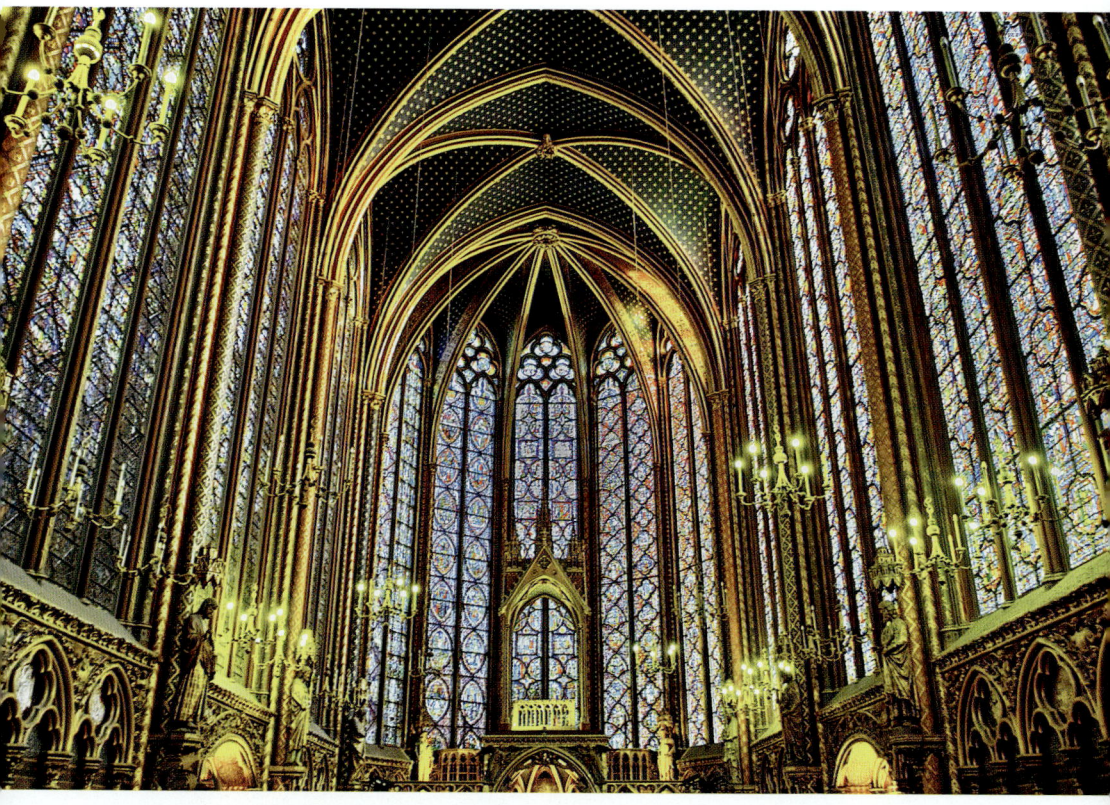

Figure 36. Sainte-Chapelle interior, built by Louis IX, 1238–48. Paris. (Photo: © Michael D. Hill Jr. / Wikimedia Commons / CC BY-SA 3.0)

preferably a Franciscan or Dominican friar who carried a letter and a reliquary along with the relic to assure its proper reception. The letter of donation from Louis stressed the importance of the gift—that it was one tiny part of the whole Crown but a great treasure, nonetheless. It also insisted upon the proper veneration of the relic, implying both physical and liturgical celebration. In response, chapels were built and a liturgy was written in Paris that was spread far and wide. Surviving inventories commemorate

Louis as the source of the relic, referring to the letters, many of which survive.

Perhaps the most remarkable part of Louis' gifting program is the inclusion of the beautiful reliquaries manufactured in Paris in which the relics were conveyed. The most spectacular surviving example is the gem-studded gold, gilded silver, and crystal reliquary in the monastery of Saint-Maurice in Agaune (fig. 37), an ancient foundation that received many royal, even imperial, gifts. Louis's contribution to this renowned treasury was delivered by Abbot Gerold of Saint-Maurice in Senlis. Remarkably, the reliquary is identical in all but a few details to a reliquary of the thorn given by Louis to San Francesco in Assisi, apparently delivered by Saint Bonaventure himself. A third reliquary in Cologne shared the basic shape and construction but was altered a few centuries later.

In each case, the thorn floats in a precisely cut ovoid of rock crystal supplied with a central cylindrical void to hold the thorn both visibly and safely. Sourced from newly available Madagascar crystal that was superior to earlier stones, the crystal is so very clear that at first glance it seems almost not to be there. In using crystal of such remarkable clarity, Louis made a point of the precise nature of his gift: the single thorn from the Crown was perfectly visible. Furthermore, although it may also refer to a heavenly surround of light, the golden, mandorla-shaped frame represents above all the unbroken ring of the Crown encircling the lone thorn. Surely this presentation also makes reference to the relic in the Sainte-Chapelle, although because its reliquary was lost in the French Revolution, we are not certain of its form. Some miniatures indicate one could see the relic inside the large Parisian reliquary, but above all the use of circular and crown shapes emphasizes the wholeness of the relic. Finally, each single thorn relic gifted by Louis and presented so precisely pointed back to its origin and, in so doing, glorified the Crown, the king, and France.

Moreover, as the cult of the Crown of Thorns radiated from Paris and developed throughout Europe, the way the circlet of the Crown came to life

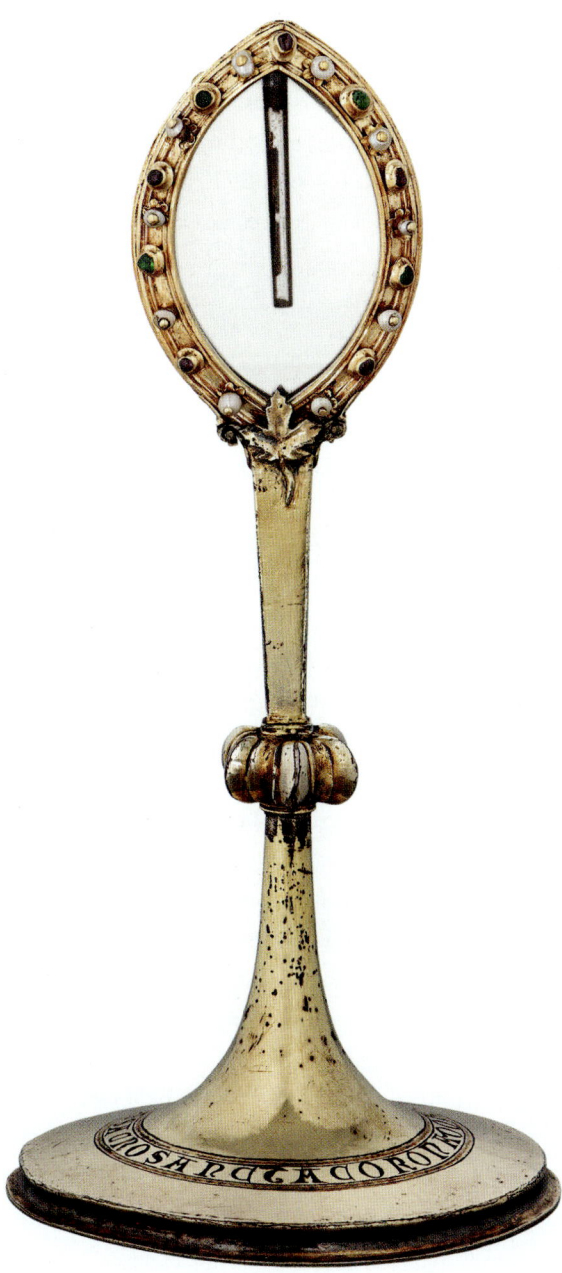

Figure 37. *Reliquary of the Thorn,* before 1262. Gold, gilded silver, rock crystal, and gems, 21 × 9.5 cm. Abbey of Saint-Maurice d'Agaune, Switzerland. (Photo: © Abbaye de St-Maurice d'Agaune / Photographers Jean-Yves Glassey and Michel Martinez)

in the imagination was even more important than its visibility. The thorn was, in effect, "taken in" and transformed in the interior of the devotee's soul as the thorn of "compunction"—that is, as a goad to contrition or the pricking of conscience. In the first decades of the fifteenth century, Thomas à Kempis, in a famous devotional text, the *Prayers and Meditations on the Life of Christ*, writes:

> Prick at last the hardness of my heart, and with the sharpest thorn on Thy head pierce its very centre; that all in my blood that is hurtful, mingled with the evils of the flesh, may pour forth from the wound and the great spur of Thy sacred love remain fixed therein. . . . And the end will be, that the rose of love will spring up in me, where once was the thorn of envy.[69]

Should we be surprised therefore when we find that pious devotees take up a particular devotion to the Crown and that some saints even receive its "marks"? In sum, as one of the foremost Passion relics, the crown became the focus of devotion and symbol of Christ's suffering. It becomes, in a sense, a frame for Christ's face, and in pictorial representations it allows a close examination of that face (as we will see in the discussion of the *Arma Christi*).

But Louis IX did not acquire just the relic of the Crown of Thorns. He obtained a full set of Passion relics that were displayed in a magnificent church-shaped reliquary on an elevated platform at the eastern end of the Sainte-Chapelle, the *Grande Châsse*, which cost 100,000 livres, again more than the chapel itself. Indeed, Louis collected portions of the True Cross, the Holy Lance, part of the vinegar-soaked sponge, the Purple Cloth, relics of the Virgin, the *Mandylion* (a miraculous cloth with an image of Christ's face), and a piece of the stone of the Holy Sepulcher, among other relics, to keep company with the Crown (see figs. 13 and 36). The platform that held the *Grande Châsse* was accessible from both sides via spiral staircases and must have been of sizeable width, as there are records of relic showings that took place upon it, and its dimensions allowed the fortunate viewer room to kneel.

*Relics of Charles IV*

One of the special guests who was privileged to visit the Sainte-Chapelle and see its relics in this fashion was a young Bohemian prince who lived with the Valois family, the future emperor Charles IV. It would seem he never forgot the power and splendor of those relics and their setting, and when he had an opportunity, he sought to create similar effects in a unique ensemble of his own. In 1333, as a young man of seventeen, Charles returned to a Bohemia that was in ruins.[70] In restoring his kingdom, he used relics and their presentation in reliquaries and churches both as a primary tool of nation building and as a means of personal self-definition as well as devotion. He consciously emulated emperors of the past such as Charlemagne and previous Holy Roman emperors, as well as members of the Capetian and Valois dynasties such as Louis IX.

Although Charles collected many relics of ancient martyrs and heroic kings, he especially treasured his collection of Passion relics. He gave many relics away to churches in his realm, especially to the Cathedral of Saint Vitus. However, in order to protect and display his most precious treasures, especially the relics of the Passion, Charles built the royal fortress and palace of Karlštejn. Located thirty kilometers southwest of Prague, it was consecrated in 1365, well before the castle itself was completed in 1372. The highest tower on the uppermost floor contained the Chapel of the Holy Cross.

The most impressive object in Charles's collection of reliquaries, once locked into this treasure room, is a cross that survives today in the Cathedral of Saint Vitus in Prague (fig. 38). Made of pure gold, the cross reveals its relics through rock-crystal windows and capsules and has lily-shaped terminals reminiscent of an earlier French style. Before commissioning the surviving cross, Charles had already created a very precious reliquary cross, but he had his cross completely remade in about 1370 after receiving an additional gift of a large relic of the True Cross from the Byzantine emperor. Charles incorporated the entire newly gifted Byzantine cross into his refashioned cross, along with two *other* relics of the Cross, one originally a gift from the French, enclosing altogether three separately sourced relic gifts of the True Cross in the reliquary.

In a Karlštejn mural in the Lady Chapel (before 1357; fig. 39), these relic donations are carefully depicted: Charles receives thorns, a gift from the French, and relics of the sponge, a gift from Duke Alois Gonzaga of Mantua. More elaborately dressed in each successive image of the fresco, Charles finally wears gilded brocades as he reverentially inserts the True Cross relic into the first version of his great relic cross. As priest-king, he steps up onto the altar's base, grasps the foot of the cross stand and, in humility, bends before the cross. It was for this cross that Charles first appealed for a papal indulgence, granted for prayers upon its display with the imperial regalia in 1357. It is, however, his second, refashioned reliquary cross that declares Charles's highest achievement (see fig. 38). Covered with exquisite sapphires, rubies, and pearls and including magnificent imperial cameos, both ancient and Byzantine, Charles's cross made the boldest possible statement: he is now emperor, displaying relic gifts from many royal and imperial sources, and his cross is ornamented with gems worthy of his status.

In his castle's Chapel of the Holy Cross, Charles sponsored what has to be recognized as one of the most beautiful and compelling of all relic ensembles. In the high tower, within the seemingly impregnable heavy-walled fortress, the chapel was probably only accessible to a privileged few, but for Charles it represented the culmination of his expression of devotion to the saints and the Passion of Christ, as well as to the empire and its heritage and rule.

One striking feature at Karlštejn is the cladding of the walls of the chapel with gold and precious gems (actually locally mined semiprecious stones and gilded *pastiglia*). Charles also literally lined the walls with saints, in painted images by Master Theodoric (fig. 40). These walls become the biblical apparition of the gemmed gates, a vision of the Heavenly Jerusalem inflected by contemporary political and spiritual exigencies. Among the

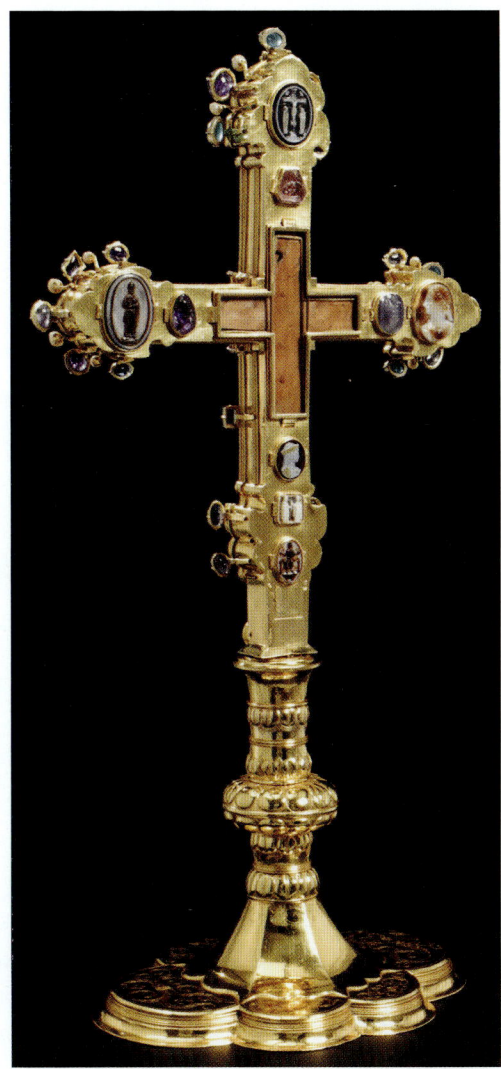

Figure 38. *Coronation Cross of Bohemia*, c. 1357, remade c. 1370. Gold, rock crystal plate, gems, and cameos. Treasury of the Saint Vitus Cathedral, Prague. (Photo: © Prague Castle Administration / Photographer Jan Gloc)

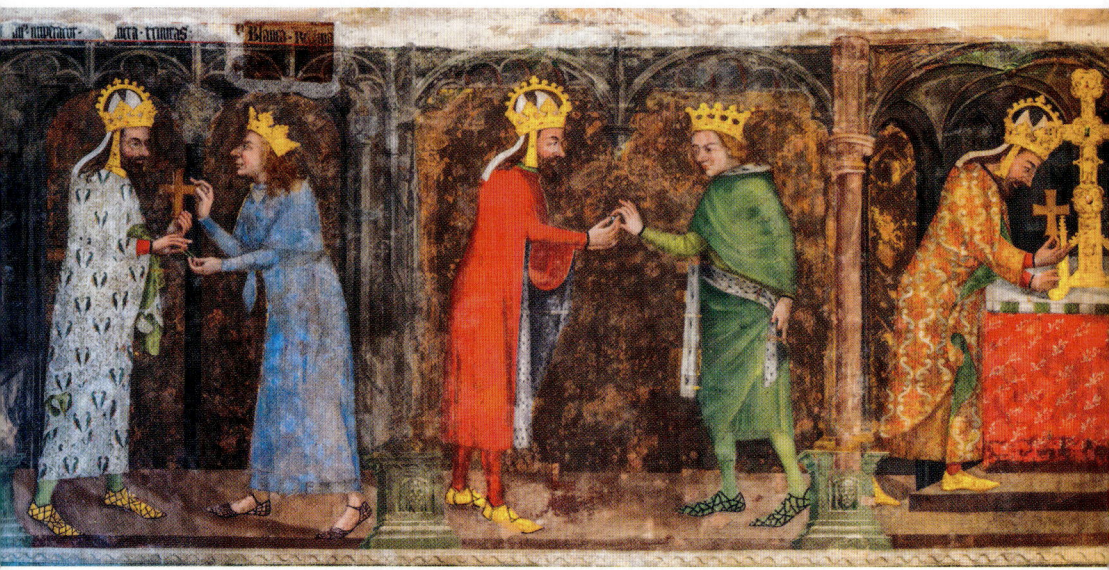

Figure 39. Nicholas Wurmser of Strasbourg, *Charles Receiving Relics of the Passion and Placing Them in the Cross*, before 1357. Wall painting. Chapel of Our Lady, southern wall, Karlštejn Castle, Czech Republic. (Photo: © age fotostock / Alamy Stock Photo)

depicted saints, whose gestures and glances create a forceful network of psychological and intercessory power within the relatively small but glorious chapel, are the Apostles and various martyrs, confessors, monks, nuns, and virgins, along with prophets and angels at the edges. In particular, one wall features Charlemagne and other emperors and knights. Each saint's portrait was made more potent with the inclusion in the lower frame of a small relic wrapped in gold foil (now removed—only the cavities remain).[71]

The altar area of the chapel has a grilled enclosure for the imperial relics, including the cross described above, and is surmounted by an image of the Crucifixion on the wall (see fig.40). The large, dark mark that is clearly visible in the center of Christ's chest today is not one of the wounds, unless we think of it as a wound to the painting. In this spot in the fabric of the

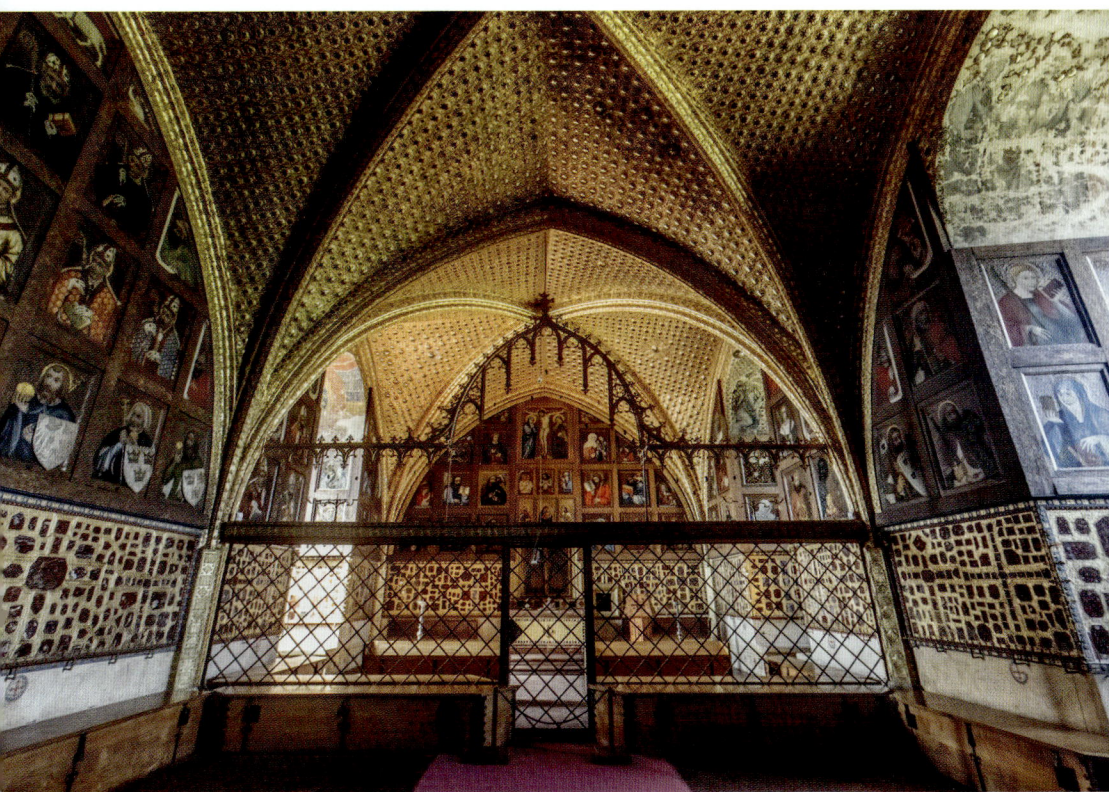

Figure 40. Master Theodoric and Workshop, Chapel of The Holy Cross, consecrated 1365. Karlštejn Castle, Czech Republic. (Photo: © Matej Divizna / Getty Images News / Getty Images)

painting were embedded two small splinters of the True Cross. Similarly, a bit of the sponge was embedded next to Christ's side wound, and a fragment of a thorn was inserted into the halo in such a manner that it pierced Christ's head. The panel constituted a second, powerful but invisible collection of Charles's Passion relics. There is no doubt that Charles succeeded beyond measure in his project of sanctifying Prague and Bohemia. His rule in Prague became the golden age, the period always remembered as the apex of the Church's prestige in Bohemia. Karlštejn remains a reminder for the Czech Republic of a proud and sanctified past.

*The Shroud and the Savoy Dynasty*

Many other collections of Passion relics are worthy of discussion: the Sancta Sanctorum in Rome, the miraculous host and other relics in Dijon, even smaller collections with perhaps only the True Cross and a thorn. I will, however, discuss only one other treasury, and in so doing, move outside the medieval era to the early modern period. Of decidedly regal aspirations, the treasury assembled at Turin Cathedral and most spectacularly celebrated in the seventeenth century contained a relic that trumped all other Passion relics: the purported burial shroud of Christ.

The Chapel of the Holy Shroud in Turin (1668–1694), according to John Beldon Scott, functioned as "an instrument for political identity formation and for state building for the Savoy [dynasty]" and was built to house a relic collection, but especially to showcase one extraordinary relic: "the only relic in Europe that still commands international attention."[72] Guarino Guarini's chapel (fig. 41) is an architectural wonder that exquisitely delivers a combination of uniqueness, artistic achievement, and political, especially royal, promotion that has been the goal of all the relic ensembles we have examined. Because of the genius of the architect and the extraordinary results of his work, the chapel does seem to be "unique" but of course many of its elements are derived from long-standing traditions of relic display.

A particularly relevant comparison to the high circular chapel at Turin with its remarkable light-filled dome that lies behind but towers over the eastern altar of the cathedral is the elevated *Grande Châsse* of the Sainte-Chapelle; in both buildings, the altar is upstaged by the relic installation. Another, much more ancient precedent for the Turin chapel is the circular plan of the Holy Sepulcher, appropriate as a model for a chapel for the shroud

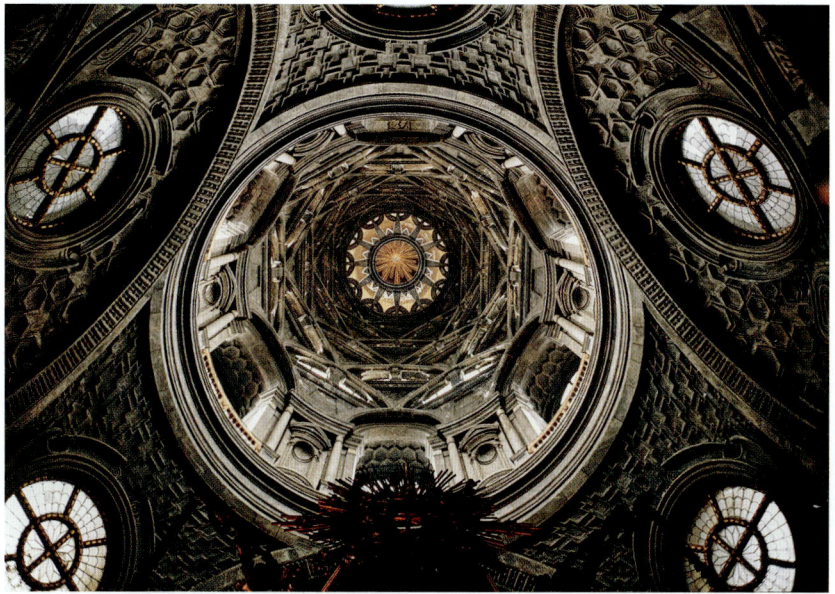

Figure 41. Guarino Guarini (architect), Chapel of the Holy Shroud (interior), 1668–94. Turin Cathedral. (Photo: © DEA / Chomon-Perino / De Agostini / Getty Images)

of Christ. The manipulation of light as in Guarini's chapel is also a feature in other relic installations. Nevertheless, even if these elements occur elsewhere, in its original disposition and extraordinary repetition and variation of forms, Guarini's ensemble was deemed by contemporaries to be "miraculous." The architect intended to "to stupefy the intellect and stun the viewer," and it too was called a reliquary in and of itself because of its preciousness and striking design. Other critics have called it bizarre and a "terror," but all viewers have noted its ability to provoke the emotions.[73]

Details of the building are no less interesting than its overall effect. Emphasizing the treasure of the Shroud as the first among all Passion relics, the bronze gilded capitals of the attached columns (highlighted against polished black marble) are articulated with images of the nails, the Crown of

Thorns, and the tablet inscribed INRI, emphasizing the presence in the treasury of other relics that literally "support" or accompany the relic that, in some sense, binds them together. Devotional exercises practiced in the chapel took the devotee systematically through the Passion story, ending with the burial and shroud as the ultimate sign of Christ's sufferings.

Perhaps the greatest of all Passion relics in its almost "narrative" quality, the Shroud displays in vividly visual terms (that is, through blood stains), the effects produced by the Passion instruments on the body of Christ. Moreover, it has remained whole, unlike the multiply splintered and disseminated Cross, Crown, or other Passion relics. Supposedly captured in battle, the Shroud first appeared in 1356, recorded as a gift to the church at Lirey from a Crusader knight, Geoffrey de Charny. The bishop of Troyes attempted to suppress a flourishing cult, and the Shroud disappeared from Charny under threat of war. It was eventually deeded to Louis, Duke of Savoy, in 1453 by Margaret de Charny—undoubtedly, money changed hands.

Like his relic-collecting ancestor, Louis IX, Louis of Savoy, inspired by Crusade-era relic prestige and his nominal claim to the Kingdom of Jerusalem, saw an opportunity and invested in it. He acquired papal certification and indulgences. The relic was offered up to view and won prestige and riches for the Savoy house. Ultimately, it was transferred to Turin Cathedral in 1572 and promoted by Louis's ducal successors. The dynasty achieved royal status in 1697, three years after the monumental reliquary chapel by Guarino Guarini was completed.

The material nature of the Shroud relic as a textile led to its exploitation in a number of exceptional practices. In its early history, it served as a battle standard, a military use comparable to the deployment of other Passion relics such as the True Cross and the lance (however those would have been enclosed in reliquaries).[74] It was occasionally referred to as a royal mantle. As cloth, it could also be stitched. In a particularly feminine form of veneration, the Savoyard duchess Anna d'Orléans repaired it following the example of an earlier, unidentified seamstress. Early modern prints feature its material nature by depicting the Shroud and its ritual display "unfurled," and a "souvenir" on fabric was even produced.

A print on silk by Antonio Tempesta (1593–1620; fig. 42) shows the press of the crowds, the excitement of the nobility, and the dignity of an ecclesiastical honor guard of seven bishops who hold up the oversize relic as the duke and duchess stand just behind them. It also shows a secondary ritual in which devotees throw special Passion rosaries, so-called *corone di Cristo*, at the Shroud hoping to transfer its power to their personal and private devotional aids. Attendants at the ends of the platform drop the rosaries back into eager, upraised arms. The Shroud itself, so difficult to see in person, almost seems to glow in this print because the miraculous image of Christ is left in reserve in a chiaroscuro effect produced by combining woodblock with engraving on the fabric. Alfonso Paleotti wrote in 1599 about seeing the Shroud:

> The celestial splendor which flashes from the most holy effigy of Christ imprinted on the Shroud is redolent of, not human, but divine artifice. Some kind of hidden energy shines out of the sheet and fills those who look upon it with heartfelt stupefaction . . . wounding the heart of the beholder with the dagger of remorse, dissolves him in tears. . . . A certain radiance in the Shroud is a thing divine.[75]

The print is very close to a tertiary or contact relic and may have been purchased within sight of the relic exhibition along with a Passion rosary; it shares in and reproduces the effect and emotion of the sight of the relic.

The Shroud had such wonderful visual possibilities precisely because of its size and "flexibility." Although it was kept in a reliquary, it did not need one to make it visible as so many relics do. As a sizable piece of cloth (14′3″ long) that "took part" in the Passion, it could be featured in iconographic renderings of the Passion: visualized as being used to lower the body into the

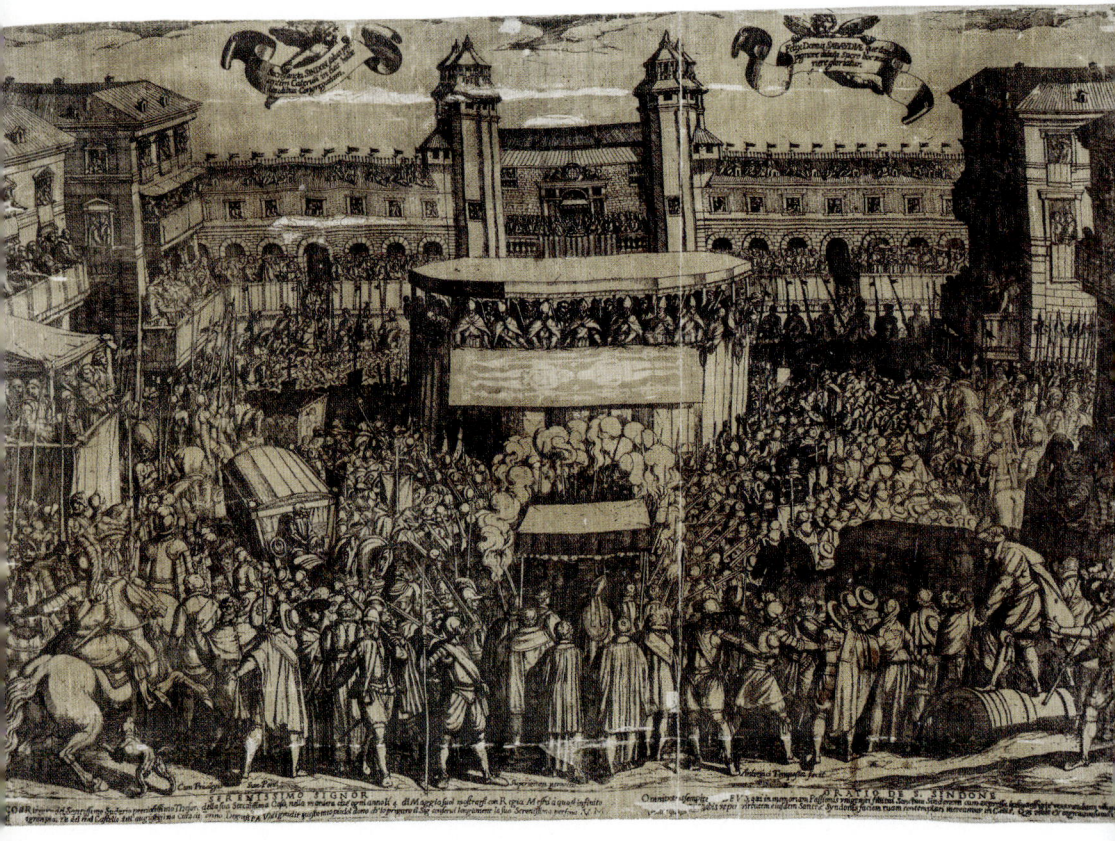

Figure 42. Antonio Tempesta, *The Annual Display of the Holy Shroud in Turin on 4 May*, after 1593–1620. Etching and woodcut printed on silk, 42.6 × 62 cm. British Museum, London. (Photo: © Trustees of the British Museum. All rights reserved.)

grave, being used to cradle the body during the pietà, or as a means for angels to transport the body after Christ's death on the cross. As a full-size image of the body of Christ, one could interact with it as Carlo Borromeo did, in veneration kissing the marks of the wounds (putatively created by contact with Christ's wounds). Members of the court were also allowed this devotion.

Thus far, we have investigated three great European collections of Passion relics. In each case we have seen how these collections were used to serve political aspirations and developed as centers of devotion. Indeed, this history can be seen as a prolonged game of one-upmanship, an attempt through relics to capture the prestige of empire through what could be called a *translatio imperii*. As Latin kingdoms collapsed in the East, Louis IX brought the inviolate and precious Crown westward, surrounded it and supported it with other Passion relics, and presented it in the most beautiful of chapels. Charles IV collected far and wide, creating an unmatched treasure trove of relics and glorified his Passion relics with a series of reliquaries and architectural spaces. The Savoy dynasty decided instead to have a particular focus. They managed to acquire the relic that, in a sense, summed up all the others, and they put it into a chapel that was recognized as a tour de force of theatrical architecture.

## DEVOTION TO PASSION RELICS

But Passion relics, although nominally owned by kings and emperors, never stayed securely in royal possession. This is not a reference to cataclysmic events such as the French Revolution, during which the Crown of Thorns passed to the Cathedral of Notre-Dame in Paris, or to the Bohemian fall from power after Charles's reign on account of which the imperial relics were moved away and later the Chapel of the Holy Cross was stripped of its relics. Rather, it is a reference to another sort of repossession: the claiming of relics by the people, by devout worshippers who in every sense made the Passion implements their own.

Such "popular repossession" could be done in many ways. One enterprising devotee touched a thorn to the Crown of Thorns and made his own relic, which he duly gave to Angers Cathedral at his death.[76] Others fashioned their own crown to wear in emulation of Christ while praying (fig. 43). Yet others stole the thorns from sculptures of the suffering Christ as

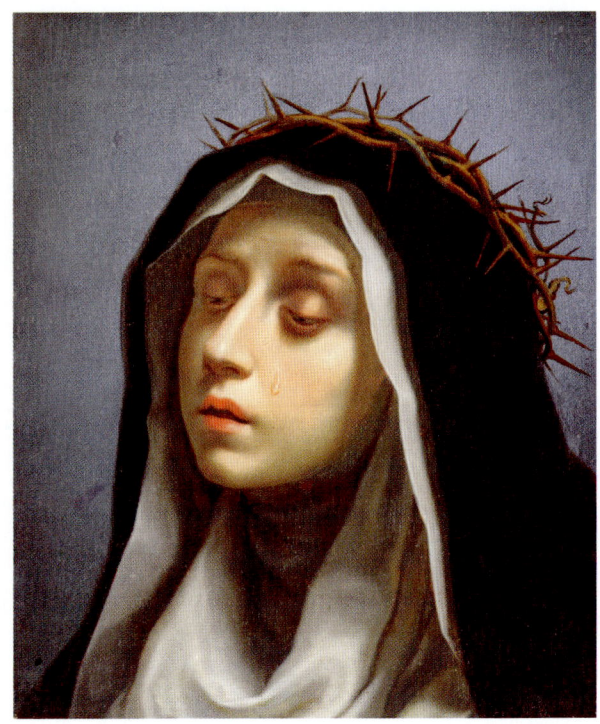

Figure 43. Carlo Dolci, *St. Catherine of Siena*, c. 1665–70. Oil on cedar panel, 24.4 × 18.1 cm. Dulwich Picture Gallery, London. (Photo: Dulwich Picture Gallery / Wikimedia Commons)

devotional mementoes to serve them in their prayers. Rita of Cascia (1381–1457), a devotee who was later declared a saint, even acquired a "wound" from such a thorn, experiencing the Crown as torment in her imitation of Christ. Souvenirs and mementoes and what are often called tertiary, or touch, relics were made for all the Passion relics, and devotees eagerly produced drawings or acquired woodcuts in order to have some sort of sensible interaction with these sacred things.[77]

More than any category of relic, Passion relics and their surrogates were a goad for the imagination, giving birth to a series of stories, elaborate devotions, and ecstatic celebrations. Such devotion began in the Early Christian period, found rich textual expression in the Carolingian and Anglo-Saxon periods, and really began to blossom with the writings of Anselm and, in his circle, John of Fécamp, who already in the eleventh century used "imaginative reconstruction through vivid mental pictures of the events of the Passion."[78] These empathetic experiences ultimately were based on the Virgin's experience of the Passion, her *co-passio,* and are remarkable for their emphasis on the visual. Here Anselm: "His naked breast gleamed white, his bloody side grew red, . . . his marble legs hung down, a stream of holy blood moistened his pierced feet."[79] In the twelfth century, the sermons of Bernard of Clairvaux established the theme of the beauty of Christ, deformed to ugliness through his torment, and Aelred's *De institutis inclusarum* urged devotees to imagine themselves present during the Passion and to experience extreme emotions.

Visual expression of these devotions in art became more common beginning in the thirteenth century, and texts multiplied. Especially notable are treatises by Bonaventure, including the *Lignum vitae* and *Vitis mystica* and others ascribed to the Franciscan saint, such as the *Meditations on the Life of Christ.* The subsequent development of Franciscan affective devotion was long-lasting and widespread. For example, Bonaventure described Christ as "our vine, the good Jesus lifted up on [the cross]" and wrote "the gnarled trunk of the vine is Christ's body twisted and deformed by the suffering of the Passion."[80] Such imagery led to a vivid perception of the divine in things and the natural world; in the eighteenth century it even led to phenomena such as the identification and cult of a miracle-working grapevine now in the cathedral museum of Valladolid (fig. 44).

## THE *ARMA CHRISTI*

Such an interrelationship of things and devotion, the imagination's need for the concrete, was essential in driving the fame and fortunes of Passion relics. Such needs, however, also led, alternatively, to image-based practices such

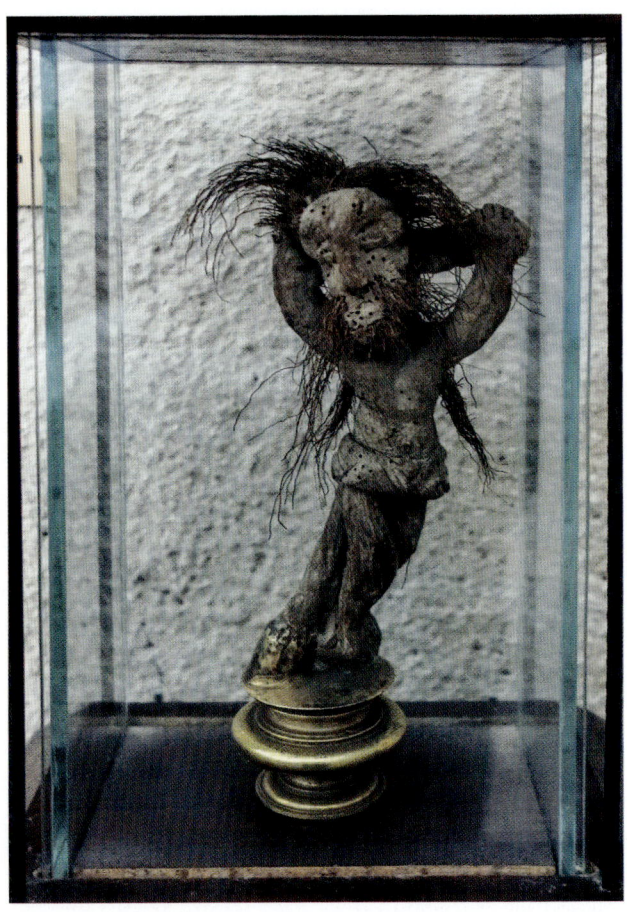

Figure 44. *Vine of Christ*, 18th century. Grapevine. Diocesan and Cathedral Museum, Valladolid. (Photo: © Cynthia Hahn)

as the devotion to the *Arma Christi*, which to some degree stand apart from relic devotion. The *Arma Christi*, as we have seen, originated in depictions of Roman battle loot but developed into specific imagery of the arms or weapons of Christ that were represented on a heraldic shield and stand for Christ's protection of his followers. In turn, the weapons came to be used by devotees to "defend" against sin and to practice contrition.

A daily martial exercise of this sort was already recommended in the fourteenth century for a devotee such as Kunigunde, a Bohemian abbess who owned the beautiful book in which one very clear depiction of the relics as weapons appears (fig. 45). Such imagery arose at the same moment and in tandem with the more general heraldry used as personal marks of identity that is still so familiar today.[81]

The specific origin of the iconography of the *Arma Christi* is still disputed. In addition to heraldic appearances, some occurrences of the collected Arms of the Passion occur in association with the relic of the Cross, as in the *Triptych Reliquary of the True Cross* (see fig. 6),[82] but they are just as often associated with the depiction of the Man of Sorrows, surely a key image for the devotion to the Passion.[83] The Man of Sorrows, or *Imago Pietatis*, originated in tenth-century Byzantium after Iconoclasm as a figure associated with the *proskomidē*, the preparation of the Eucharist.[84] In its transfer to the West, the gut-wrenching, explicit image of a suffering body became not the dead but the miraculously upright Christ, a figure that returned the gaze of devotees and displayed not only his wounds but also the instruments of the Passion. It is an image that demands interaction and, as Mitchell Merback argues, has "a capacity to organize exchanges and compel reciprocities."[85] It need not be associated with relics.[86]

Flora Lewis argues that three elements served to drive the rise of such devotions. Relics and indulgences interacted with prayer regimes, all working together to promise salvation. The Veronica set a precedent—as both relic and image, its veneration escalated after an indulgence in 1216 granted by Innocent III.[87] Given that indulgences were at first usually associated with relics rather than images, Lewis proposes that the popularity and prestige of the Passion relics in the Sainte-Chapelle in Paris may have played a very important part in winning another indulgence, that for the image-based

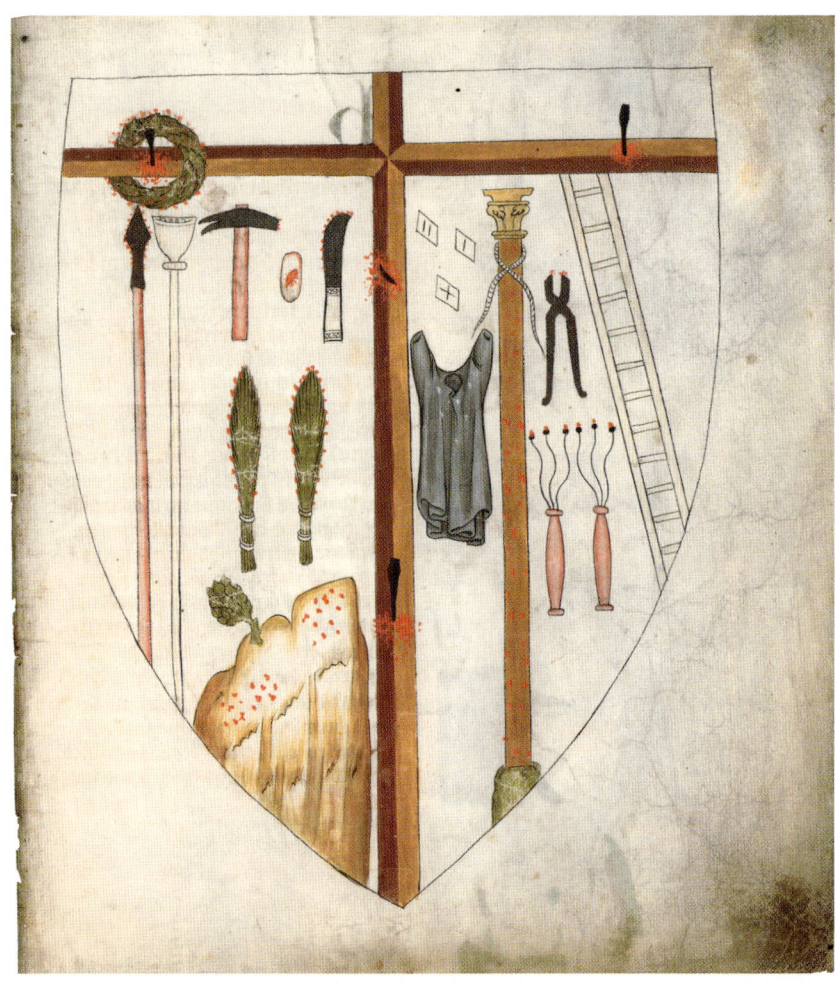

Figure 45. "Arma Christi," in Kolda of Koldice, *Passionale of Abbess Kunigunde*, XIV.A.17, fol. 3r, 14th century. Manuscript, 30 cm × 25 cm. National Library of the Czech Republic, Prague. (Photo: © National Library of the Czech Republic)

devotion to the *Arma Christi*. It was granted by Innocent IV in 1240 at the Council of Lyon.[88] The Man of Sorrows itself became an indulgenced image but may have been associated with the so-called Mass of Saint Gregory, which was linked to the miniature mosaic icon of the subject surrounded by relics that is now in Rome.[89] Rather than a single source, the rise of devotion to the *Arma* seems to have been motivated by many more or less simultaneous cultural developments.

One example is telling. A reliquary of the Man of Sorrows (1347–49), in a variant standing position, was created to celebrate a major gift to the emperor Charles IV of a relic of the thorn (fig. 46).[90] The reliquary also held relics of the Cross and the column and served to bring these tiny fragments together in a gorgeous but touching evocation of the suffering of Christ through the use of the implements of torture. Displaying and presenting the divine body that was tormented but then resurrected, as in the Byzantine ivory with which we began (see fig. 20), shows the torture turned to victory. Here the thorns prick, but they produce not pain and blood but a shining ruby to crown Christ the king. The thorn itself would have been displayed in the tiny coffin-shaped container in the front of the multipart reliquary.

The *Arma Christi* represented here, through both relics and images, was above all an extraordinary prompt to elicit devotion. In attempting to understand its dynamics, we should not be satisfied with a simplified model of interaction. Instead, as Flora Lewis argues, story led to metaphor, led to object, led to sense perception, led to devotion, and cycled back through story and object again. The circulation, or semiosis, of ideas and meanings acted much like the fluidity of associations described in chapter 1 concerning the Cross, although perhaps it was even more freewheeling and productive.

In a text that records her visions and devotions, the *Legatus divinae pietatis*, the thirteenth-century German mystic Gertrude of Helfta supplies an example of this sort of extraordinarily precise, complex, and imaginative use of an image—in this case using the Veronica image that was created

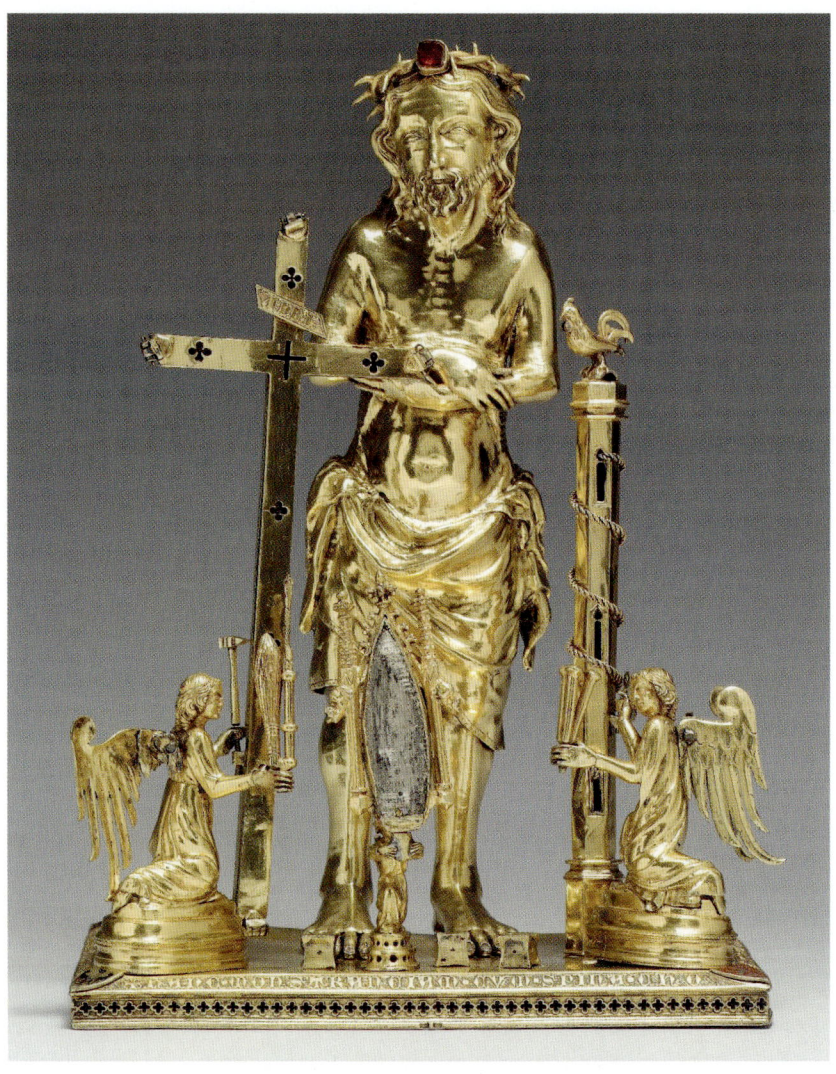

Figure 46. Bohemian artist, *Reliquary with the Man of Sorrows*, commissioned by John Volek, Bishop of Olomouc (1334–51), 1347–49. Gilded silver, silver, champlevé enamel, and glass paste (imitation ruby), 29.5 × 21.3 (width at wings) × 12.7 cm. Walters Art Museum, Baltimore, Maryland. (Photo: Walters Art Museum / Wikimedia Commons / CC BY-SA 3.0)

miraculously from the sweat of Christ's face as he carried the cross and was therefore also a relic. In its medieval "copies," it rarely took the same form, although was always just a "face" (fig. 47).

Gertrude used it as a focus for devotion in which she performed spiritual confession. Despite its abbreviated form, the nun used the image as a prompt for an imaginative trajectory that led her on a pathway of prayer beginning at Christ's feet. Then she reverenced his hands (neither appear in Veronica images, only in her imagination), and finally ended at his "most loving face."[91] Jeffrey Hamburger explicates the interaction with the image: "The Veronica is both an image and a relic; the face it depicts, like Christ himself, is at once ugly and beautiful, an emblem of the Incarnation and Resurrection. As a figure of a twofold transformation—Christ's passage from heaven to earth and back again—the veil [the cloth the image is imprinted upon] stands for the ultimate mystery, promise, and paradox of Christian faith; the general resurrection of the dead."[92] Ultimately Gertrude's ambition is to recover God's image in her soul in anticipation of a hoped-for future vision of the face of God after death.

Although, the *Arma Christi* work most often as a group, prayer rituals such as Gertrude's can use one image from the collection to launch a multipart devotion. Alternatively, devotees frequently focused on single objects from the group, contemplated in succession in an extended process of prayer like "O Vernicle." That devotional poem, however, although treating each element separately, again ultimately emphasizes the aggregate force of the *Arma*.

In either approach, the senses are the binding elements of such devotions, and they are consistently invoked in prayers from the *Ancrene wisse* to "O Vernicle."[93] Even Jacobus de Voragine emphasizes Christ's multisensory experience of the Passion in order to elicit response in kind from the devotee.[94] As Kathryn Rudy describes, the manuscripts that contained such texts and images could be literally battered and dirtied by the passionate kissing and touching that was aroused by the sensory response to them.[95] To

## De tempore

**Superueniens t‍amen uestis ad hoc sudarium fecit.**

Credentes sese iesum recepta‹...› ypa‹...› occultare. Cum uero festinali‹...› statim **De ueronica** regina anglie casibus ‹...› eisd‹...› auctenti‹...› cione. cura solicitabatur effigie uult‹...› dn‹i›. et ueronica dia‹...› ut mensis de ea. s‹ed› p‹er› ‹...› ad hospit‹...› s‹anc›ti isp‹...› ueniens ‹et› post‹...› baulabat. qua p‹at›ea. i‹p›a effigies d‹omi›ni. loco suo ‹...› daretur se p‹er› seculari ut illo stabat op‹er›te. ita ut ‹...› inferius barba sup‹er›ius locar‹et›. Q‹uo› nimis abhorrer‹...› credide‹runt› illud i‹n› tribu sibi p‹re›sagii euenisse. Et pleni ‹...› golauer‹...› ostio ft‹...› thomæ ipsi‹us› effigiei que veronica ‹...› q‹uo›d d‹omi›n‹u›s oculis eor‹um› opuisse‹...› cui abicebit oculi psalmi‹...› ‹...› a usua‹...›. Et eade‹m› dicitu‹r› dies ‹...› e‹...› indulgentie. Sc‹...› ut o ‹...› septua‹...› e‹...› repetiu‹...› ‹...› dicta cum a‹...› indulg‹en›e de gene‹...› ‹...›gila igne eloque‹n›tie et p‹re›ce‹...› memorie com‹m›endetur. ut co‹...› maior‹...› acs‹...› de vocis p‹re›dic‹...› effigiaui‹...› hoc m‹od›o.

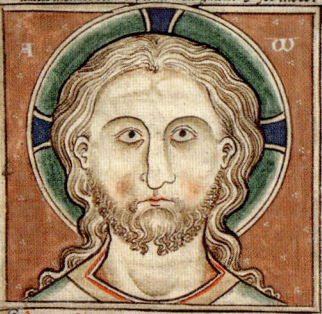

**Oratur a‹u›t ueronice taliter, n‹omi›ne ‹...› q‹uo›d mulier se d‹eo› a‹...› ‹...›genitum ipa‹m› fecit. i‹p›e i‹p›am imp‹re›ssit. Signat ‹et› se ho‹...›**
Signacu‹...› ‹et› nos d‹omi›ne ‹...› psalm‹...› ut du. Ky‹rielei›s‹on›. ‹...›
resp‹onde›t. hoc ps‹alm›s. fac me‹...› signu‹...› Ne‹...› Tu‹...› dir‹...› fac‹...› ‹et› cu‹...› sc‹...› Quere cetu‹...› i‹n› du‹...› Ad. ¶ Ora‹...› nob‹is› V‹er›o‹n›ic‹a›. R. D‹om›i‹n›e ex‹audi› o‹rati›o‹nem› m‹eam›. A‹lius› d‹eu›s u‹irtut›‹...›.

**D**eus qui nob‹is› signati lumine uult‹us› tui ‹...›
me‹m›or‹iale› tuu‹m› ad i‹n›stantia‹m› ueronice sudario ipressi ymag‹...› relinque uoluisti. p‹er› passione‹m› ‹et› crucem tua‹m› tibi nob‹is› ‹...› ut cu‹m› die ‹...› tres p‹er› spec‹...› ‹et› enig‹m›ate ‹...› aduare ‹et› ueniari ualeam‹...› i‹n› facie ad facie‹m› uenire‹...› te ‹et› seu‹...› te iude‹...› e‹...› min‹...› regnat ‹...›

**C**om‹m›issa a‹...› sie hist‹...› p‹ri›ncipal‹...› ‹...›anuale‹...› re‹...› C‹um› rana‹...› ‹...› ad lodoui‹...› ‹...› ei‹us› ‹...›gunt spe‹...› di‹...› ‹...›re homi‹n›‹...› reue‹...›. Discurre‹...› ‹et› a nulla ‹...›ia ab i‹n›cult‹...›. p‹ec›u‹ni›a ex‹...› d‹...› ‹...› debach‹...› Walte‹...› gesie theuto‹...› n‹...› i‹n› ore magno pla‹...› cum s‹...› mulio‹n›‹...› ‹...›rili‹...› resiste‹...›. Multo‹rum› a‹n›i‹m›as ex ga‹...› ligenti‹...› ex‹com›‹m›unicat‹...› ad tartara‹m› direx‹er›‹...› s‹ed› de nec p‹ost› diut‹ur›na‹m› obsidione‹m› ‹et› preceptu‹m› regis dict‹...› Waltera‹n›‹...› ‹...› placet et lodouico castellum salui tibi equi‹...› ar‹m›is reddider‹...›. xiii. ‹kalendas› ianuar‹ii›. **I**ncrasti‹...› ‹...›no aute‹m› ip‹...›stat s‹unt› i‹n› castello lodouic‹us› uenit ad sc‹...› albanu‹...› i‹n›die uidelic‹et› beati thome apli‹...› rogant ab ‹...› ut faceret sibi homagiu‹...›. S‹ed› cum abbas

respo‹n›disset se nolle et homagiu‹...› facere nisi prius absolueretur ab homagio q‹uo›d fecerat regi anglo‹rum›. Lodouic‹us› uehementer indignatus iurauit se igne p‹er›tota‹m› albacia‹m› cum uilla cotta cremati‹...› nulla facer‹...› quo‹...› pe‹...›bat. Tande‹m› abba‹s› p‹re›dict‹...› post p‹er›monit‹i›o‹n›e‹m› ‹et› r‹...›‹...› interuenientib‹us›. co‹m›ite Winton‹...› sine fecit. p‹er› se tul‹...›la rota da‹n›s Lodouico p‹ro› i‹n›duciis usq‹ue› ad p‹ur›ificatio‹n›e‹m› beate marie ‹quingentas› marcas argenti. Anno ‹...› Lodouic‹us› ad urbe‹m› Lond‹...› reuersus est. **Incidentia de cru‹ce›.**

Eodem anno expirante treuga int‹er› fideles ‹...›tres punit‹...›‹...› ‹et› Saracenos. In p‹ri›mo passagio generali post jugulum lazara‹n›e‹n›se. congregatus est exercit‹us› d‹omi›ni copiosiss‹imus› i‹n› achon cum tribu‹s› regib‹us›. tertia laudis hungarie ‹et› egypti. Affuer‹unt› ‹et› duces Austrie. ‹et› Ma‹...›raucie cum miliciis magni regni theutonic‹orum› ‹et› com‹...›ualis universus q‹...› genero‹...›. Affuer‹unt› ratishei‹...› i‹n› chostentis iouenensis auguste‹nsis›. hungarie. batoceuses ba‹...›uergenses. aucomenses. monasteriensis. ‹et› tale‹n›sis. Et al‹ii› ui‹r›i nobiles ac potent‹es›. Walter‹us› de auen‹...›. Deinde p‹...› archa ieroslimitam cum magna humilitate cleri ‹et› ip‹...› tolle‹runt› reuerencia‹...› uincl‹...› crucis lignum. feria sexta p‹er› festu‹m› om‹n›ium sc‹an›c‹t›‹orum› p‹re›fert‹ur›. ‹et› ab achon d‹omi›ni usq‹ue› ‹...› p‹or›tarerunt ad ciuodam‹...›. Hoc auc‹m› d‹omi›ni crucis lignum post uita‹m› ho‹...› reseruatu‹m› fuit ad hec tempo‹ra›. q‹ua› fideles occultau‹...›. Imminente e‹...› co‹n›flictu sarace‹...›nor‹um› tempore sala‹...›dini. cu‹m› xp‹istian›i fl‹...› a seruob‹...› ‹...›cu‹...›erit. cr‹uci›s feria sit‹...› ciuli p‹ar›s ab celu‹m› u‹...›va. et ibidem p‹...›itia. p‹ar›s tempore reseruata exiuit q‹...› t‹...› e‹...›chiber‹...›. c‹...› tali quoq‹ue› ux‹...›illo a diebus instruxit. p‹...›ferunt fideles per a‹n›num sate usq‹ue› ad forte‹m› tuba‹n›nu‹m›. eo die multa ‹sa›luauim‹us›. L‹...› p‹...› nullis expla‹n›antib‹us› uide‹ntes› ab aduersariis ‹...› mutati p‹...›iu‹n›t. in‹...›ua fuer‹...› u‹...›i contra nos an fugie‹...›do p‹...›atar‹...›. Sequenti die a‹...› montes gelboe quot habuerant ad dextra‹m› ‹et› paludum. ‹et› ad sinistra‹m›. p‹...›fu‹...›sunt hech‹...›a‹n›a ubi aduersari‹us› i‹n› ‹...›‹...› ‹et› i‹n› casta memo‹...›‹...› enr‹...› ad uitam tam copiosa‹...› dei iuuente cr‹uci›s ‹...› tam ordinate p‹ro›cedente‹...›. temoa‹...› tollent ‹et› fugient. iam mil‹...› ub‹...› xpi uastanda reliqu‹...›. Vnde i‹n› anglia s‹e›d m‹ar›tini lo‹...›da‹n›t transeu‹n›t‹es› corpa sua l‹...›uer‹unt› i‹n› eo fideles. ‹et› pacific‹...›qu‹...›um‹...› ibidem p‹er› biduu‹...›. u‹...›iali‹...› copia‹m› repe‹...›runt. Deinde sup‹er› lit‹...›us‹...› mare gal‹i›le‹...› ad natio‹n›es pagines lo‹...›. i‹n› qu‹a› saluator‹...› n‹oster› mirabili‹a› opati dignat‹...› est. copiali p‹...›entia cu‹m› tu‹mu›ltus comitatu‹...›. Aspexer‹unt› h‹...›bardam ciuitate‹m› andre‹...› ‹et› p‹ro›p‹er› i‹n›d‹e› ad modicu‹m› casale relaxat‹...›. uider‹unt› et lea ubi xp‹istu›s discipulos u‹oca›uerat. supra mare t‹y›bica‹...› pedib‹us› a‹m›bulauit i‹n› det‹...›‹...› turbat paue‹...›. mo‹n›te e‹...›cauit asce‹n›dit. L‹...› p‹ost› resurrectione‹m› eum discipli‹...› ma‹n›ducauit. L‹...› sic p‹er› capharnau‹m› i‹n› achon reuersi sunt i‹n›firmos suos reporta‹n›t‹es›. Deinde alia‹m› equitatione‹m› aggressi‹m› fideles p‹re›dicta. p‹er›cxer‹unt› ad monte‹m› thebe‹...›. ubi p‹ro› aquar‹um› inopia ‹et› p‹...›noduli deso‹...›lati p‹...›os reperier‹unt›. Hespaba‹n›t aut‹em› capita‹n›ei exercit‹us› de ascensu mo‹n›tis. donec du‹...› s‹...› est c‹astrum›› suu‹m› q‹...›chen c‹...› stile a pu‹...›to sarraceno. Con‹...›lui‹t› ergo ir‹...›e‹...› et dn‹s› pa aduent‹...›is cu‹m› leg‹...› eu‹n›gli‹...› i‹n› castell‹...› ego co‹n›fit‹...›

further explore the wide range of textual and representational prompts, we will focus on the possibilities of one of the instruments because it can serve to indicate the possible effects of such multisensory devotion.[96]

## The Lance Again

As noted above, in the story of the Passion, the wound in Christ's side was made by the lance wielded by the soldier Longinus. In that the wound emitted both water and blood, it was understood to represent both Christ's death as well as baptism and Eucharist. Given the profound significance of the wound, perhaps it is no surprise that the weapon that caused it rose to prominence among the Passion relics and their devotions.

Various material iterations of the lance, again as noted above, appeared as early material instances of Passion relics and were even realized as liturgical implements (see fig. 27). Remarkably, the lance relic seems also to have been understood as a fitting relic for rulers. In effect, it was transformed into a spiritual weapon in service to Christian kings. Many of the relics of the Holy Lance were associated with royal or imperial collections in Paris, in Constantinople, and in Vienna.

The Viennese lance is a particularly telling example of the active nature of the relic ( see fig. 28). It was customarily kept inside the imperial cross along with a large True Cross relic. It always seems to have been a weapon or tool at the same time that it was a relic *and* a reliquary: the lance was wrapped in sheet gold and silver to honor it, leaving, however, its original form visible and its function intact. It was used actively throughout its history, I would argue, to reproduce its actions and their significance. For example, it multiplied itself through fragments incorporated into other "lances" (again, therefore, lance-shaped reliquaries) and produced secondary relics through

Figure 47. "The Veronica," in Matthew Paris, *Chronica Maiora II*, CCCC MS 16, fol. 53v, 13th century. Vellum manuscript, 35.8 × 24.4 cm. Parker Library, Corpus Christi College, Cambridge. (Photo: © Parker Library, Corpus Christi College)

the action of piercing the vellum—that is, skin. We should also recall that lances were frequently pictured as weapons to guard the sacred, as at Christ's tomb in the Toulouse châsse (see fig. 17).

These are the aspects of the lance as object and implement that particularly stimulate its operation in terms of imaginative devotion. In one of the first texts discussed above, it was turned as a weapon against Hades. In the Utrecht Psalter, it is wielded against a suffering martyr (or the Psalmist himself), who through his suffering drops the chains of sin (fig. 48).[97] We have noted its appearance in the hands of angel guards in scenes of the Last Judgment.

In later medieval devotional literature and art, as one of the most important arms or weapons of *Arma Christi*, the lance came to be strongly associated with Christ himself figured as knight and lover.[98] Modeled on the knight of courtly fiction who rescues his lover from danger and wins her back, in these literary and illustrative depictions, Christ wins the love of the Christian soul through his knightly virtues, and his weapons are an intrinsic part of his identity. One text has Christ enjoin:

> At the entrance to the chamber hang my shield
> Fix my lance near your bed,
> And then you will have no fear of any adversity.[99]

The text reminds us that the arms together, especially in heraldic mode, as displayed on a shield, function as protective, even amuletic, signs (see fig. 45). But the lance at bedside is suggestive, indicating particular protection for the body and its boundaries.

Like the active cross in the "Dream of the Rood," the weapons "show" and tell:

| | |
|---|---|
| Spere and cros, nail det[y] and þorn | (Spear and cross, nail [unclear] and thorn |
| Schewen hou I bouthte man þat was forlorn[100] | Show how I saved man that was forlorn) |

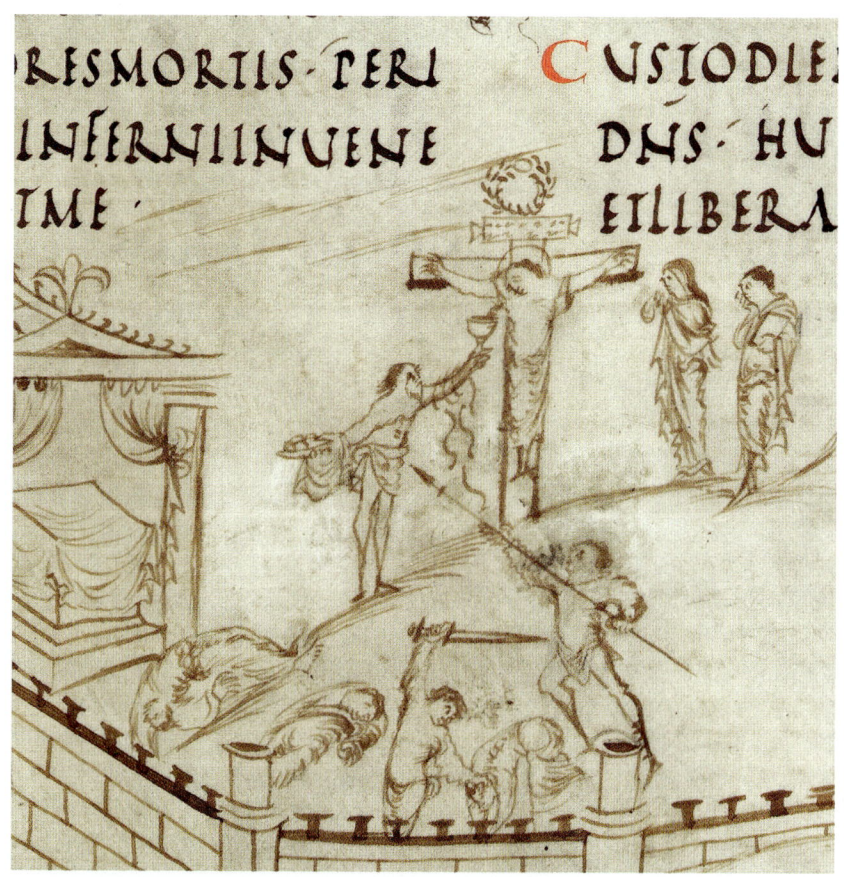

Figure 48. Detail of illustration for Psalm 114/115, *Utrecht Psalter*, Ms. 32, fol. 67r, c. 820–35. Manuscript, 33 × 25.5 cm. Utrecht University Library. (Photo: © Utrecht University Library)

And in a text, the *Parabola*, about Christ as knight and lover that is included in the Prayerbook of Kunigunde, each weapon has its own moment in the story. In explicating the Passion through its instruments, the devotional writer Kolda focuses on the lance and the wound that it made. In an illustration of this passage, Kunigunde is pictured adoring the wounded Christ (fig. 49). The scene recalls the story of the doubting Thomas and its focus on touch, as well as the feminine version with Mary Magdalene, the *Noli me tangere*. True to the latter, Kunigunde makes no physical contact. The spear also makes no contact, but stands to the right of the images, erect and unmoving but with a halo of red blood around its sharp tip, standing as witness to its wounding action and its profound import.

In a more dynamic interaction of devotee, story, and lance, the female *sponsa*, or devotee "married" to Christ, wields the lance in the *Rothschild Canticles*, a compilation of devotional texts (fig. 50, p. 116).[101] The action takes place across the gutter of the manuscript, across an opening of two miniatures, but again, no contact is made. Christ points invitingly to his side—in what is a markedly confined space, he almost seems to dance among the other instruments of the Passion: the Cross, the column, the bindings, the Crown, the nails, and the flail (fig. 50, p. 117). Furthermore, the sensory dimension of the paired miniatures is heightened by the way the *sponsa* touches her veil, as if she were reluctant to look at the nude figure of Christ exposed before her, perhaps she prepares to receive a revelation that will overwhelm. The image is excruciatingly intimate, almost sexual, and that same sensation is heightened in a somewhat later devotional text.

In the much-copied thirteenth-century devotional text by Eckebert of Schönau, the *Stimulus amoris*, the prayer to the lance is spoken by a man rather than a woman: "O si fuissem loco illius lanceae, exire de Christi latere noluisse, sed dixissem: Haec requies mea in saeculum saeculi" (Oh, if only I would have been in the place of that spear, I would have refused to go out of the side of Christ, but would have said: Here I will remain for ever and ever;

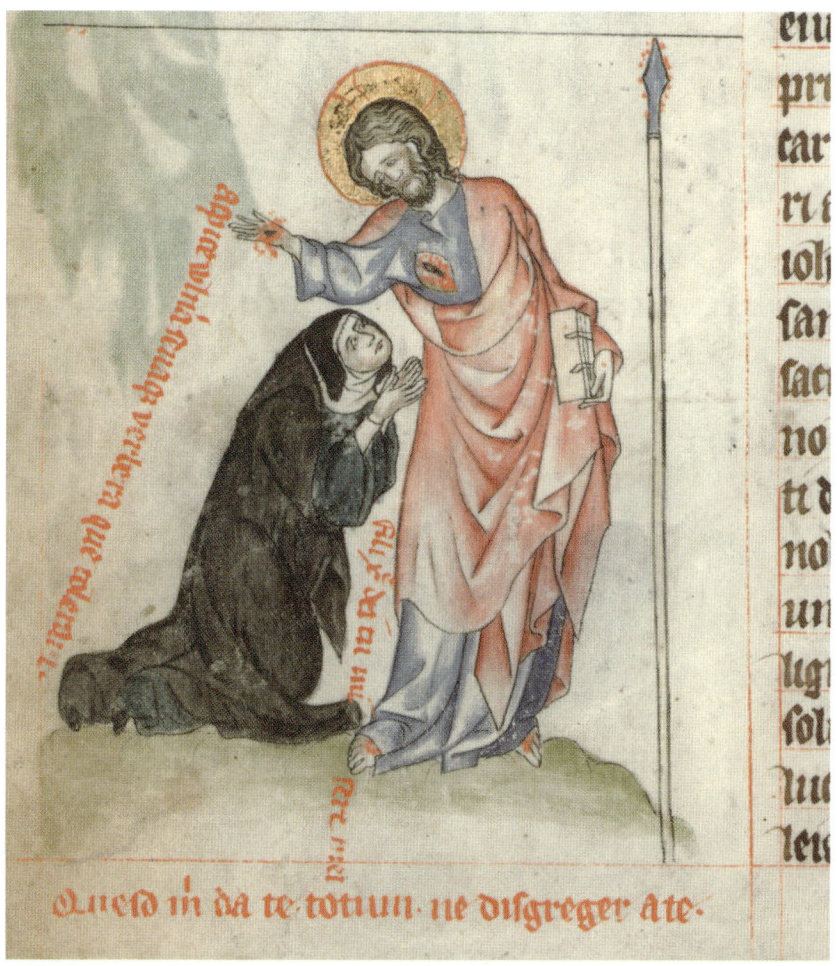

Figure 49. "Kunigunde before Christ, the Lance," in Kolda of Koldice, *Passionale of Abbess Kunigunde*, XIV.A.17, fol. 7v, 14th century. Manuscript, 30 cm × 25 cm. National Library of the Czech Republic, Prague. (Photo: © National Library of the Czech Republic)

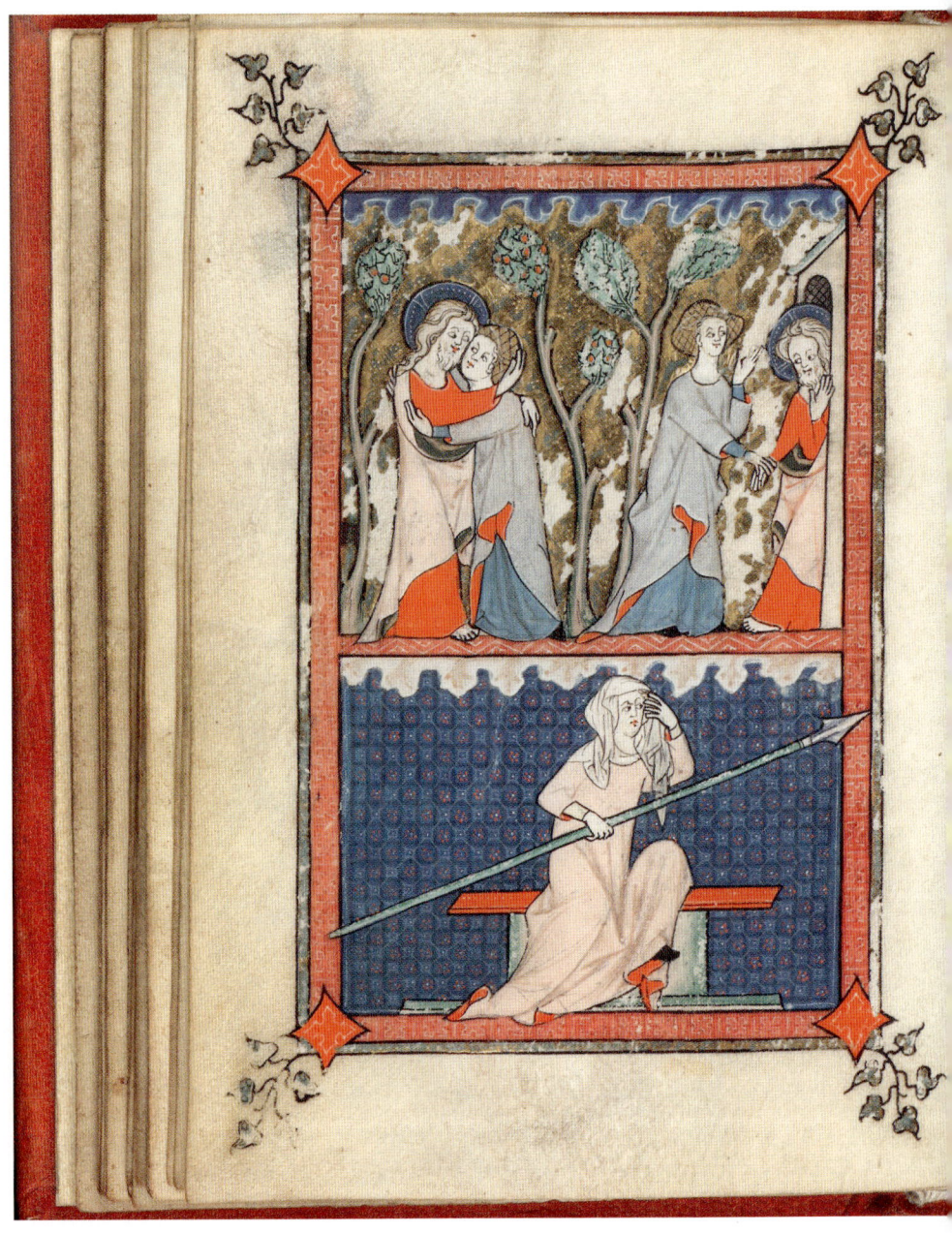

Figure 50. "Sponsa and Man of Sorrows," in *Rothschild Canticles*, MS 404, fol. 18v and fol. 19r, 14th century. Manuscript, 11.8 × 8.4 cm. Beinecke Rare Book and Manuscript Library, Yale University, New Haven, Connecticut. (Photo: Beinecke Rare Book and Manuscript Library)

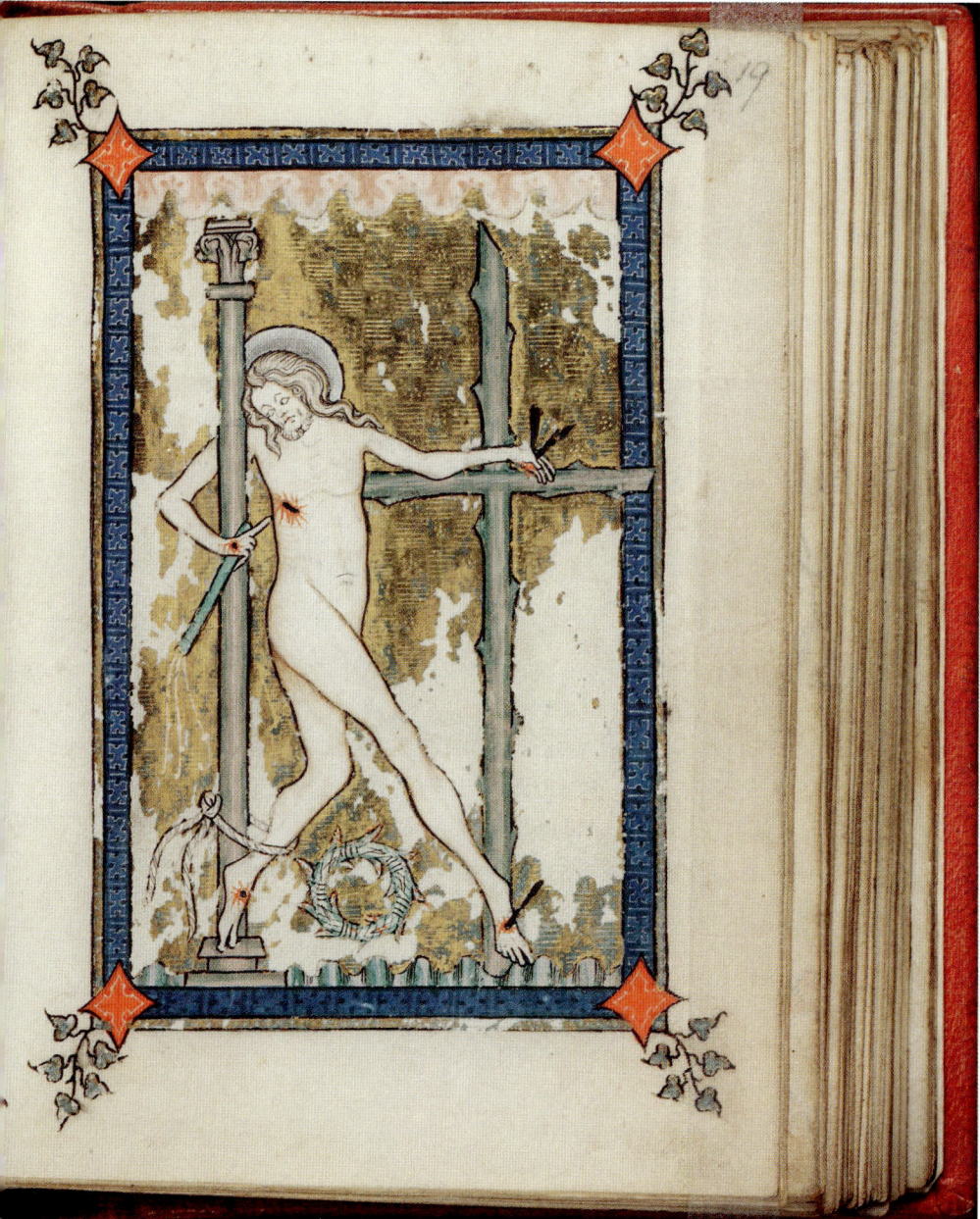

(referring to Ps. 131:14).[102] This passionate request to rest forever, in the form of the spear, in the side of Christ is surely a strange image to us. Nevertheless, it is one that reifies the desire to get ever closer, to touch and even examine Christ's wounds, Christ's skin. This is an urge that ultimately presages the later devotional imagery of the Sacred Heart.[103] In that final leap of intimate devotion, the devotee prays to enter the body, the heart, even the bowels of Christ in what is almost a "return to the womb."[104]

## CONCLUSION

In sum, beginning in the early Church but gaining force in the eleventh century, a closely linked interest in devotion, imagery, relics, and, by the early thirteenth century, indulgenced prayer led to practices that brought increasing prestige and importance to relics of the Passion, especially those in the great royal and imperial collections (whose owners often sponsored the indulgences). These collections began an assertive relocation of the holy through time and space—scattering "New Jerusalems" across Europe and creating proliferating centers of sacred power.

Devotional practices continued the relocation, allowing a colonization of the religious imagination by these powerful instruments of empathy. The cross provides the vital field of action, the lacy and prickly crown frames the story and presents the face of Christ, the nails pierce and fix, creating empathetic pain and riveting memory in the form of blunt iron but allowing action in the world—of the limbs:

| | |
|---|---|
| Þe nayles thoro fete and handes two | (The nails through feet and hands two |
| Þei help me out of sinne and wo | They help me out of sin and woe |
| Þat I haf in my lif do | That I have in my life done |
| with handes I handelid, with fet I go[105] | with hands I handled, with feet I go) |

The lance protects and pierces as well as empowers the devotee. Similarly, the scourge, sponge, and ropes complement and further the narrative; the column provides the measure; and the clothes and shroud wrap and comfort the devotee.

Above all, Passion relics (even the tiniest fragment or even a simulacrum) excited the soul with the presence of the sacred and set off a chain reaction that released the devotee to ever more rarefied flights of the imagination in prayers intended to lift the soul heavenward. In their materiality and presence, Passion relics may seem to have "captured" the divine, but it was the working of the devout mind and the Christian imagination that found a way to God.

# NOTES

In citing works in the notes, short titles have generally been used. Works frequently cited have been identified by the following abbreviations:

PG        Migne, Jacques Paul. *Patrologiae cursus completus / Patrologia Graeca: . . . omnium ss. patrum, doctorum, scriptorumque ecclesiasticorum, . . ., sive Graecorum, qui ab aevo apostolico ad aetatem Innocenti III (ann. 1216)*. Multivolume work. Paris, 1869 and other editions.

PL        Migne, Jacques Paul. *Patrologiae cursus completus / Patrologia Latina: . . . omnium ss. patrum doctorum scriptorumque ecclesiaticorum . . ., Series Latina*. Multivolume work. Paris, 1878 and other editions.

## INTRODUCTION

1. Bynum, *Christian Materiality*.
2. And a few bits such as the foreskin, which under some circumstances could also be considered a Passion relic because the circumcision is the first shedding of blood. Discussed in Steinberg, *Sexuality of Christ*, 50.

## CHAPTER ONE. THE LURE OF PASSION RELICS, THE POWER OF THE CROSS

1. Calvin, *Treatise on Relics*, 234.

2. Drijvers, *Helena Augusta*, 82, citing *Catechesis* X, 19, *PG* 33, cols. 685–87, https://archive.org/details/patrologiagraeca33/page/n341.

3. Holum, "Hadrian and St. Helena," 66–84. I sum up the story of Helena as it was accepted in the high and later Middle Ages. The early textual tradition is complicated and contradictory. See Jensen, *Cross;* and Drijvers, *Helena Augusta*.

4. Eusebius tells the story in his *Life of Constantine*, bk. 1, ch. 28, reported to him by Lactantius (www.newadvent.org/fathers/25021.htm). See Barnes, *Constantine and Eusebius*, 30–31.

5. Klein, *Byzanz;* Baert, *Heritage of Holy Wood;* and Hahn, *Strange Beauty*, ch. 5.

6. This is close to a literal translation of the Vulgate. We recall that the "place of propitiation" was sprinkled with the blood of a sacrificial lamb to allow God to forgive sins (Lev. 17:11). For the window, see Crosby, *Royal Abbey*, 86.

7. Legends tell that the True Cross derives from a tree from Paradise. For these legends, see Jacobus de Voragine, *Golden Legend*, and Baert, *Heritage of Holy Wood*.

8. Friede, "Time and Eternity," 363–76; George, "'Sur la terre comme au ciel'"; Verdier, "Les staurothèques mosanes," especially 99–102 on angels.

9. As Schiller emphasizes, the showing of the wounds derives from Zechariah 12:10. Schiller, "The 'Arma Christi,'" especially 188.

10. See the discussion of how the *Arma Christi* functioned in this fashion in the next chapter. A related triptych in Liège adds the nails to the same collection of *Arma*. Berliner, "*Arma Christi*."

11. Hahn, *Portrayed on the Heart*, 68.

12. Similarly, in a Cranach painting of Luther preaching, an image of the Crucifixion materializes before his audience. Jensen, *Cross*, 182–83.

13. The first quote comes from Eusebius, *Life of Constantine*, ch. 29, the second from ch. 31 (http://www.newadvent.org/fathers/25021.htm). I thank Brigitte Buettner for discussing this text with me. For another story of conversion through the sign of the cross, see the discussion of Albinus in Hahn, *Portrayed on the Heart*, 291–93.

14. Ivan Foletti has also observed this quality; he cites earlier bibliography in "The British Museum Casket."

15. De Blaauw "Following the Crosses."

16. Amalarius of Metz, as noted by Chazelle, *Crucified God;* Amalarii episcopi 2, 102: "Quamvis omnis ecclesia non eam possit habere, tamen non deest eis virtus sanctae crucis, in eis crucibus quae ad similitudinem dominicae crucis factae sunt." Translation from "The Cross and Crucifix in Liturgy," *Catholic Encyclopedia* online, www.newadvent.org/cathen/04533a.htm.

17. Peers, *Sacred Shock*, 13.

18. Peers, *Sacred Shock*, 25, citing the monk Dadisho, *Treatise on Solitude and Prayer*, a Syriac text of the seventh century from the monastery of Rab-Kinnaré. Translation from A. Mingana, "Dadisho," 136.

19. Van Tongeren, *Exaltation of the Cross*, 2. Much of the subsequent discussion of the feast comes from this book.

20. For celebration of Exaltation of the Cross in Constantinople, see Klein, "Constantine," especially 35-38.

21. Van Tongeren, *Exaltation of the Cross*, 184-85.

22. Van Tongeren, *Exaltation of the Cross*, 186.

23. The very extensive bibliography on the "Dream" includes Fleming, "Dream of the Rood," Chase, "'Christ III'"; Mahler, "Lignum Domini"; Holloway, "Dream of the Rood"; Ó Carragáin, *Ritual and the Rood;* and Carruthers, *Craft of Thought*, 169-71. The quotations from "Dream of the Rood" are from the translation by Elaine Treharne, *Old and Middle English Anthology*, www.apocalyptictheories.com/literature/dor/medora1.html.

24. Jensen discusses the cross talking, and even walking. *Cross*, 28-29, 189.

25. Fleming, "Dream of the Rood," 70. See articles by Gerevini and Toussaint on rock crystal in *Seeking Transparency*, ed. Cynthia Hahn and Avinoam Shalem (Berlin: Reimer Verlag, forthcoming).

26. Szövérffy, "'Crux Fidelis,'" especially 25-26.

27. Chazelle, *Crucified God*, 60, citing *Adv. Felicem* 7.8, *PL* 101.220 A-C.

28. Chazelle, *Crucified God*, 42, a sentiment expressed in Theodulf, *Opus Caroli regis*, 102, ll. 14-17.

29. Ladner, "St. Gregory of Nyssa," especially 90 and 91.

30. Chazelle, *Crucified God*, 163, citing the Carolingian text of Candidus Bruun, *De passione Domini*, 19, *PL* 106.98D, 101. Peers makes a similar argument in *Sacred Shock*, 29, citing Ode 42 in the second-century *Odes of Solomon* (Charlesworth, *Odes*, 143-46):

I extended my hands and approached my Lord,
For the expansion of my hands is His sign.
And my extension is the common cross,
that was lifted up on the way of the Righteous One.

31. Drijvers, *Helena Augusta*, 133; and see Drijvers, "Promoting Jerusalem." Also see Wharton, *Selling Jerusalem*.

32. Drijvers, *Helena Augusta*, 82, citing *Catechesis* X, 19, PG 33, cols. 685–87.

33. Letter 31.6 in Walsh, *Letters of St. Paulinus*, 132–33.

34. The column included an array of relics including the Cross and the crosses of the two thieves. John Cotsonis, *Byzantine Figural Processional Crosses*. See Klein, "Constantine"; and Wortley, "Legend of Constantine."

35. Scholars dispute this. Jensen, *Cross*, 66.

36. Klein, "Eastern Objects."

37. See Hahn, *Strange Beauty*, ch. 5, for further discussion.

38. Gaposchkin, "Place of Jerusalem"; see also Gaposchkin, "From Pilgrimage to Crusade"; and Gaposchkin, *Invisible Weapons*.

39. Wall, *Relics of the Passion*, 60.

40. He goes on to clarify by saying, "but not the image of the nails or of any such thing." Aquinas, *Summa Theologica*, Question 25, art. 4, www.newadvent.org/summa/4025.htm#article4.

41. Frolow, *Relique de la Vraie Croix*.

42. Hahn, *Strange Beauty*, 81; Hahn, "Collector and Saint."

43. They may have been made by Western artists, whose presence is documented in the Holy Land. Folda, *Art of the Crusaders*, 27–28; Kühnel, *From Earthly to Heavenly Jerusalem*, passim.

44. Meurer, "Andenken und Geschenke," 42.

45. Meurer, "Stauroteken der Kreuzfahrer," 66: "sollten alle, die ein Kreuzfahrt gelobt hatten, diese jedoch ohne eigenes Verschulden nicht antreten konnten, gegen Gebet und Gütershenkung an die Grabeskirche von ihrem Gelübde gelost." Nikolas Jaspert, "Gedenkwesen und Erinnerung."

46. Hahn, "Collector and Saint."

47. Thuno, *Image and Relic*.

48. Klein, *Byzanz*, 226–29; Boehm, *Enamels of Limoges*, 165–66, no. 40; Watin-Grandchamp et al., "Le coffret reliquaire"; Jaspert, "True Cross."

49. Jaspert, "True Cross," argues this represents the institution of a prayer brotherhood.

50. MacCormack, *Art and Ceremony*; Gussone, "Adventus-Zeremoniell."

51. I have found Catherine Fernandez's dissertation, "Quidem lapis preciousus," extremely useful in understanding the Crusader importance of Toulouse.

52. Shagrir, "Visitatio Sepulchri."

53. The frescoes were dated by style to the 1180s, but an inscription discovered in 2007 has changed the thinking on this and the other frescoes of the "Passion" group that are associated with the Easter liturgy. Piano, "Passió de Crist," links them to liturgical reforms under the Augustinian canons from the time of the dedication of the church. Durliat, "Théophanies-visions," and Lyman, "Theophanic Iconography," at an earlier moment, argue for the date in the 1180s and for association with visions and/or the Easter liturgy.

54. The frescoes are currently under restoration, and the photographs available to me are very imperfect. A close examination of the soldiers in the frescoes will have to be delayed. It must be admitted that there is substantial damage in this section and if the frescoes date to 1118, they may be related only in a very general way to the châsse; nevertheless, if the canons ordered the châsse, they may have been inspired by these associations, especially liturgical aspects.

55. The other two shields are marked with crosses made of spears with fleurons or lilies attached. None is the so-called Toulouse cross, or the typical Chi-Rho.

56. Duffy, *Stripping of the Altars*, 25ff.: "Angels" were also important parts of this drama and its depiction, which may explain the presence of two angels with an empty speech scroll in the peak at one end of the reliquary. The other small end holds a depiction of the Annunciation. The Angels bearing crowns in the *Majestas* scene are also a significant addition. Klein, *Byzanz*, 226–29, has suggested that the crowns are the holy rewards for the two main protagonists from Toulouse, Raymond and Pons, and that the casket was not made until after their deaths as commemoration. Douais, "Deux reliquaires," 166 and 169, argues that the relic was divided as there are three crosses listed in an inventory of 1246, although the coffer itself is not mentioned.

57. In storage, #902-1905, or consult the Victoria and Albert Museum website, http://collections.vam.ac.uk/item/O68889/the-resurrection-panel-unknown/.

58. Victoria and Albert Museum Collections, *Tabernacle*, #7650-1861, http://collections.vam.ac.uk/item/O81507/tabernacle-unknown. Discussed more fully in Hahn, "The Toulouse Reliquary of the True Cross and the Transfer of the Holy," in *Projections of Jerusalem in Europe: A Monumental Network*, ed. Bianca Kühnel, Renana Bartal, and Neta Bodner, forthcoming.

59. Most of the following account of Count Raymond of Toulouse is told with many more details by historian Jonathan Riley-Smith in *First Crusade*.

60. The description of the reception of the lance benefited from hearing William Purkiss, "The Making and Unmaking of Relics in the First Crusade," at the Medieval Academy meeting of 2015 at Notre Dame. I look forward to his book to be published by Yale University Press.

61. Riley-Smith, *First Crusade*, 98. A story explains that Orthodox priests had hidden the relic and that Arnulf had to torture them to reveal their secrets. Jensen, *Cross*, 174, citing Steven Runciman, *History of the Crusades*, 1:294.

62. Arnulf was quickly replaced as patriarch and made archdeacon but then recovered the post in 1112. Spear, "School of Caen."

63. Gaposchkin, *Invisible Weapons*, 182–83.

64. Gaposchkin, *Invisible Weapons*, 142.

65. Jaspert, "Gedenkwesen und Erinnerung," 168–74, analyzes all the entries in Arxiu Diocesà de Barcelona, Fons de Santa Ana, ND-1; also see 164–65 for liturgical celebrations and reminiscences of the Holy Sepulcher in the West.

66. Gabrieli, *Arab Historians*, 136–37. See also Murray, "'Mighty against the Enemies.'"

67. Gabrieli, *Arab Historians*, 136–37.

## CHAPTER TWO. PASSION RELICS: STRENGTH IN UNITY

1. Scarry, *Body in Pain*, intro.

2. Jacobus de Voragine, *Golden Legend*, 2:168.

3. Rohault de Fleury, *Mémoire*. See also Wall, *Relics of the Passion*, which relies on Rohault de Fleury.

4. Rohault de Fleury, *Mémoire*, 89–163, discusses cross measurements with a series of tables of sizes by volume of cross fragments.

5. Rohault de Fleury, *Mémoire*, 207.

6. Rohault de Fleury, *Mémoire*, 169.

7. Areford, *Viewer and the Printed Image*, ch. 5.

8. Berliner, "*Arma Christi*," especially 39; and Lansdowne, "Broken but Not Divided."

9. Edsall, *Arma Christi*, 32

10. Frank, "Death in the Flesh."

11. Jensen, *Cross*, 69–73, discusses this sarcophagus and emphasizes its relationship to the story of the Apostles indicated by the outermost scenes.

12. Schiller, "'Arma Christi,'" 2:186.

13. Translation of Latin in Schiller, "'Arma Christi,'" 188.

14. For reliquaries with Passion relics, although not the lance or nails, rather the foreskin and cross, see Gaborit-Chopin et al., *Le trésor de Conques*, 32–36, 52, 54. Other instances of imagery correlating to treasury holdings include the Lateran mosaic, which might evoke the contents of the Sancta Sanctorum, and the portal of Sainte-Chapelle with its Crown of Thorns; see discussion later in this chapter.

15. The number of nails is discussed in Rohault de Fleury, *Mémoire*, 165–67.

16. Bynum, *Christian Materiality*.

17. In what is a very scholarly treatment, Chiara Mercuri is determined to track a single object in *Corona di Christo*. In contrast, Berliner's list of Passion relics is succinct and speaks to the proliferation of relics c. 1400. Berliner, "*Arma Christi*," 37–38.

18. The best discussion of the various True Cross legends is Drijvers, *Helena Augusta*.

19. Hewitt, "Use of Nails." The nail relic was also multiplied because, as various apologists argue, other nails were used in the *making* of the cross.

20. Chaganti, "Figure and Ground," 53–82.

21. Hewitt, "Use of the Nails," 42.

22. Merback, *Thief, Cross and Wheel*, 97; Berliner, "*Arma Christi*," 44; and Jensen, *Cross*, 79.

23. Engemann, "Zur Verbreitung."

24. Thiofrid of Echternach, *Flores epytaphii sanctorum*, quoted in Berliner, "*Arma Christi*," 40.

25. Bestul, *Texts of the Passion*, 41.

26. The translator comments that the word *boisterous* seems inappropriate and replaces it with *coarse*, as noted by Scarry, *Body in Pain*, 328, n13; and Merback, *Thief, Cross, and Wheel*, 76, argues that this nail "speaks" its pain.

27. Such legends may originate in special pleading for Constantine as Christian ruler. Bojcov, "Der Heilige Kranz."

28. Wall, *Relics of the Passion*, 115.

29. Conti, "Crown"; Bertelli, "From Crown to Relic"; Elbern, "Iron Crown of Monza"; and Pillepich, "Napoleon and the Iron Crown."

30. Westermann-Angerhausen, "Das Nagelreliquiar."

31. And the nail in Siena was important to civic ritual: Shaw, "Peace-Making Rituals."

32. Wall, *Relics of the Passion*, 118; also see the rather exhaustive description in Rohault de Fleury, *Mémoire*, 165–82. Schulze-Dörrlamm, "Heilige Nägel und heilige Lanzen," compares surviving relics to archaeological examples, especially bridles and lances. At 1:153–62, there is a list of objects and relics as they are documented chronologically.

33. "Nevertheless, may you rejoice greatly with great joy, now that you are glorified by him in heaven, who was fixed in your mind most bitterly by nails of a most holy death." Ogier of Locedio, *Quis dabit,* quoted in Bestul, *Texts of the Passion*, 166–69. One nail was reputed to be fixed in the vault of the Duomo of Milan, according to Bromley, *Remarks*, 45. Another nail is recorded in Milan in c. 1200, which Bojcov, "Der heilige Kranz," 66, notes may be a Crusader artifact.

34. Wall, *Relics of the Passion*, 40.

35. Nagel and Wood, *Anachronic Renaissance*, ch. 19.

36. Hahn, "Inscriptions and Interactions." Only one other major relic of the *titulus* is noted by Wall, *Relics of the Passion*, 102, listed as "Notre-Dame in Toulouse." As there are three churches dedicated to the Virgin in the city, it is not clear which is intended.

37. Schiller, "'Arma Christi,'" 190.

38. Lansdowne, "Broken but Not Divided."

39. Schulze-Dörrlamm,"Heilige Nägel und heilige Lanzen," 1:157–59.

40. Kirchweger and Wolf, *Die Heilige Lanze*.

41. Berliner, "*Arma Christi*," 40.

42. Kirkpatrick, *Hitler's Holy Relics*.

43. Schiller, "'Arma Christi,'" 194–95.

44. Schier and Schleif, "Seeing and Singing," especially 418.

45. Willems, *Der hl. Rock*; Wikimedia has a useful article (along with others on the *Arma Christi*): https://en.wikipedia.org/wiki/Seamless_robe_of_Jesus.

46. Wilmowsky, *Der Dom zu Trier*; Aretz et al., *Der Heilige Rock*.

47. "Der 'Heilige Rock,'" Bistum Trier, http://www.heilig-rock-wallfahrt.de/start.html.

48. Kaegi, *Heraclius*, 188–89.

49. "Geißelsäule" in Wikipedia (German) is an especially informative page: https://de.wikipedia.org/wiki/Gei%C3%9Fels%C3%A4ule. Also see "Geißelsäule" in *Lexikon der christlichen Ikonographie*, Freiburg: Herder, 1970, 2:126.

50. Schiller, "'Arma Christi,'" 188.

51. Whitman, "Transfers of Empire," 913.

52. Caroline Bynum has discussed the topic thoroughly in *Wonderful Blood*.

53. Vincent, *Holy Blood*. The bishop of Norwich claimed it was holier than Louis's cross relic. See Bynum, "The Blood of Christ," 693.

54. Heinlen, "Early Image"; and Saalman, Ghirardini, and Law, "Recent Excavations."

55. Merback, "Fount of Mercy"; Underhill, "Fountain of Life," especially 100. Also see Fricke, "Liquid History."

56. Bacci, "Berardenga Antependium."

57. For example, a text that focuses the imagination on the "sheddings" of blood and even counts the drops is Hennessy, "Disappearing Book"; see also Hennessy, "Social Life of a Manuscript Metaphor," for another understanding of that blood.

58. Listed in Gregory of Tours, *Gloria Martyrum*, 1:5, and others. See also Lidov, "Byzantine Jerusalem," 78.

59. Lidov, "Byzantine Jerusalem."

60. Klein, "Eastern Objects and Western Desires." Charlemagne is said to have asked for relics rather than riches in *Le Pèlerinage de Charlemagne*. Burgess, *Pilgrimage of Charlemagne*; Horrent, *Le Pèlerinage*, 39–45.

61. Note the discussion of the Bruges blood relic earlier in the chapter, in the section "Holy Blood." See, among others, Paul and Yeager, *Remembering the*

*Crusades*, especially the introduction; and Cassidy-Welch and Lester, *Crusades and Memory*.

62. Pastan and Balcon, *Les vitraux*, 186–87.

63. For discussions of this text and Charlemagne, see Fernandez "Quidem lapis preciosus"; Pastan "Charlemagne as Saint?"; Hahn "The Sting of Death"; and Burgess, *Pilgrimage of Charlemagne*, 39, which discusses a nail specifically from Christ's foot. However, these relics were probably those said to have been given to Saint-Denis by Charles the Bald in *Descriptio qualiter Carolus Magnus clavum et coronam Domini a Constantinopoli Àquisgraai adtulerit, qualiterque Carolus Calvus hec ad sanctum Dionysium retulerit*. This text was written at Saint-Denis in the eleventh century. Paris, "La chanson du *Pèlerinage de Charlemagne*," especially 34–36. Sometimes rulers follow Charlemagne's example quite literally. For example, see the story of Henry the Lion's purported gifts from the emperor of Constantinople and his pilgrimage to the Holy Land in Ehresmann, "Iconography of the Cismar Altarpiece," especially 28.

64. Burgess, *Pilgrimage of Charlemagne*, 39.

65. The list of the top ten religious relics in *Time* magazine begins with Turin Shroud and includes the chemise and belt of Mary but also includes the beard and footprint of the Prophet and Buddha's tooth. The list is more political than even the hierarchy of Rohault de Fleury. Kayla Webley, "Top 10 Religious Relics," *Time*, April 19, 2010, http://content.time.com/time/specials/packages/article/0,28804,1983194_1983193_1983100,00.html.

66. Burgess, *Pilgrimage of Charlemagne*.

67. See Branner, "Grand Châsse"; and Cohen, *Sainte-Chapelle*. Also for the relics and reliquaries, see Durand and Avisseau-Broustet, *Le trésor de la Sainte-Chapelle*.

68. Hahn, "Sting of Death."

69. From "the great spur of thy sacred love remain fixed therein," Thomas à Kempis continues: "till I be fully purged from the thorns of vice, and the thistles of temptation, and so duly prepared for the seeds of virtue. Thus may the ground of my heart, infected with the first curse, by the infusion of Thy sacred Blood, receive a new blessing. And the end will be, that the rose of love will spring up in me, where once was the thorn of envy; the lily of chastity, in place of the nettle of lust; the violet of humility, instead of the briar of vanity; and the flowers of

gentleness where once flourished the brambles of asperity. Amen." Thomas à Kempis, *Meditations*, 104–5. Is it a coincidence that the thorn here is paired with the lily, a prominent part, as the fleur-de-lis, of the French royal coat of arms?

70. Bibliography on the relic collections in Prague and Karlstein includes Boehm, "Charles IV"; Crossley, "Politics of Presentation"; Fajt, *Magister Theodoricus*; Fajt and Royt, "Pictorial Decoration of the Great Tower"; Homolka, "Pictorial Decoration of the Palace"; Opačić, "Sacred Topography"; and Suckale and Fajt, "Circle of Charles IV." Also see Hahn, *Reliquary Effect*.

71. These included authentics, but this bishop remains anonymous. Fajt, *Magister Theodoricus*, 518.

72. Scott, *Architecture for the Shroud*, xxi, xxii. Scott's treatment is brilliant and I rely upon it in the discussion of the Turin Chapel and the history of the relic.

73. Amedeo di Castellamonte called the chapel a terror: Scott, *Architecture for the Shroud*, 136, 191, 214.

74. See Scott, *Architecture for the Shroud*, fig. 18.

75. Scott, *Architecture for the Shroud*, 116.

76. Mély, *Exuviae sacrae constantinopolitanae*, 362; Leclerq dates the Angers document to the fourteenth century. Cabrol and Leclerq "Instruments de la Passion," *DACL* VII, cols. 1149–61, especially 1156, https://gallica.bnf.fr/ark:/12148/bpt6k34122553/f593.item.

77. Hamburger, *Nuns as Artists*.

78. Bestul, *Texts of the Passion*, 37. One wonders where to insert such warped mirrors of Christian devotion as the legend of the Beirut blood. In that story, an image of Christ was tormented just as his body was during the Passion, and the result was that the image bled and created miracle-working relics. See Bacci, "Berardenga Antependium."

79. Anselm, *Orationes sive meditationes*, quoted in Bestul, *Texts of the Passion*, 38.

80. Paraphrased in Bestul, *Texts of the Passion*, 46.

81. Dennys, *Heraldic Imagination*. Also see discussion of the *Scutum fidei* in Kumler, *Translating Truth*, 76–81.

82. In these collections, the Passion instruments are the focus of meditation, linked with a Mosan interest in the virtues and care for the soul, especially among the clergy; they may represent the origins of the devotion to the *Arma*. See

Hahn, "Portable Altars"; the Passion instruments already appear on the Liège triptych and Klosterneuberg altarpiece (mentioned in this chapter) and even earlier in the illustrations of the Thiofrid of Echternach's *Flores epytaphii sanctorum* quoted in reference to the nail. For an image see Hahn, *Strange Beauty*, 24, fig. 11. Also see Schiller, "'Arma Christi,'" 187–88 for this general question of the early development of the *Arma Christi*.

83. Belting, "An Image and Its Function"; and Merback, "Man of Sorrows."

84. Lansdowne, "Broken but Not Divided."

85. Merback, "Man of Sorrows," 78.

86. For an introduction to one example that includes relics, see Bertelli, "*Image of Pity*."

87. Lewis, "Rewarding Devotion," especially 179.

88. Lewis, "Rewarding Devotion," 178–81.

89. Parshall, Schoch, et al., *Origins of European Printmaking*, 262. The mosaic icon is discussed in Bertelli, "*Image of Pity*"; and Lansdowne, "Broken but Not Divided."

90. Bagnoli et al., *Treasures of Heaven*, 205–6; Tammen, "Dorn und Schmerzensmann"; and Berliner, "*Arma Christi*," 63.

91. Hamburger, "Frequentant memoriam," especially 231.

92. Hamburger, "Frequentant memoriam," 238. This article is the most thorough explication of a Passion relic devotion that I have read. Also for finding the self in a devotional image, see Merback, "Man of Sorrows." For a range of practices, see Hennessy, "Disappearing Book"; and Hennessy, "Social Life of a Manuscript Metaphor."

93. Astell, "Retooling the Instruments," especially 181; and "O Vernicle," in Cooper and Denny-Brown, *Arma Christi*, for example, 360.

94. Jacobus de Voragine, *Golden Legend*, 2:168.

95. Rudy, "Kissing Images."

96. Much of this discussion of relic devotions and indulgenced images is dependent on Flora Lewis's work as well as the classic studies Berliner, "*Arma Christi*"; and Suckale, "Arma Christi." Suckale also emphasizes the multivalent nature of the relic devotions. See also Lewis, "The Wound"; and Lewis, "Rewarding Devotion."

97. This image has more of a reason to be associated with the *Arma Christi* than does the other, more conventional assemblage of weapons in the Utrecht

Psalter (see fig. 23). It includes the titulus, cross, lance, and crown above the cross. It has never, so far as I know, been discussed in this context but probably should be linked to the triumph of the Church.

98. Woolf, "Theme of Christ the Lover-Knight."

99. Lewis, "The Wound," 218.

100. Lewis, "The Wound," 210. Thanks to Marlene Hennessy for help with this text.

101. Jeffrey Hamburger, *Rothschild Canticles*, 72.

102. Lewis, "The Wound," n46.

103. Already present in Bonaventure, *Vitis mystica*, as noted in Bestul, *Texts of the Passion*, 48.

104. Lewis, "The Wound," 216; and Merback, "Fount of Mercy."

105. These lines suggest that the prayers release the body for action. "O Vernicle," in Cooper and Denny-Brown *Arma Christi*, 368

# BIBLIOGRAPHY

Areford, David. *The Viewer and the Printed Image in Late Medieval Europe.* Farnham, UK: Ashgate, 2010.

Aretz, Erich, Michael Embach, Martin Persch, and Franz Ronig, eds. *Der Heilige Rock zu Trier: Studien zur Geschichte und Verehrung der Tunika Christi.* 2nd ed. Trier: Im Auftrag des bischöfl. Generalvikariats, Paulinus-Verlag, 1996.

Astell, Ann W. "Retooling the Instruments of Christ's Passion: Memorial Technai, St. Thomas the Twin, and British Library Additional MS 22029." In Cooper and Denny-Brown, *Arma Christi*, 171–202.

Bacci, Michele. "The Berardenga Antependium and the Passio Ymaginis Office." *Journal of the Warburg and Courtauld Institutes* 61 (1998): 1–16.

Baert, Barbara. *A Heritage of Holy Wood: The Legend of the True Cross in Text and Image.* Translated by Lee Preedy. Leiden: Brill, 2004.

Bagnoli, Martina, Holger A. Klein, C. Griffith Mann, and James Robinson. *Treasures of Heaven: Saints, Relics, and Devotion in Medieval Europe.* Baltimore: Walters Art Museum, 2010. Issued in connection with an exhibition at Cleveland Museum of Art, Walters Art Museum, and British Museum. Distributed by Yale University Press.

Barnes, Timothy D. *Constantine and Eusebius.* Cambridge, MA: Harvard University Press, 1981.

Belting, Hans. "An Image and Its Function in the Liturgy: The Man of Sorrows in Byzantium." *Dumbarton Oaks Papers* 34–35 (1980): 1–16.

Berliner, Rudolf. "*Arma Christi.*" *Münchner Jahrbuch der bildenden Kunst* 3 Folge, Band 6 (1955): 35–152.

Bertelli, Carlo. "From Crown to Relic." In Buccellati, *Iron Crown*, 2:15–32.

———. "The *Image of Pity* in Santa Croce in Gerusalemme." In *Essays in the History of Art Presented to Rudolf Wittkower,* edited by Douglas Fraser, Howard Hibbard, and Milton J. Lewine, 40–55. London: Phaidon, 1967. Part 2 of Essays Presented to Rudolf Wittkower on His Sixty-Fifth Birthday.

Bestul, Thomas H. *Texts of the Passion: Latin Devotional Literature and Medieval Society.* Philadelphia: University of Pennsylvania Press, 1996.

Boehm, Barbara Drake. "Charles IV: The Realm of Faith." In *Prague: The Crown of Bohemia,* edited by Barbara Boehm and Jiří Fajt. New York: Metropolitan Museum of Art, 2005.

———, ed. *Enamels of Limoges: 1100–1350.* New York: Metropolitan Museum of Art, 1996.

Boehm, Barbara D., and Jiří Fajt, eds. *Prague: The Crown of Bohemia 1347–1437,* New York: Metropolitan Museum of Art, 2005.

Bojcov, M. "Der heilige Kranz." *Frühmittelalterliche Studien* 42 (2008): 1–69.

Bromley, William. *Remarks Made in Travels through France and Italy with Many Publick Inscriptions.* London, 1693.

Branner, Robert. "The Grand Châsse of the Sainte-Chapelle." *Gazette des Beaux-Arts* 77 (1971): 6–18.

Buccellati, Graziella, ed. *The Iron Crown and Imperial Europe.* 2 vols. Milan: G. Mondadori, 1995.

Burgess, Glyn S., ed. and trans. *The Pilgrimage of Charlemagne = Le Pèlerinage de Charlemagne.* Introduction by Anne Elizabeth Cobby. New York: Garland, 1988.

Bynum, Caroline W. "The Blood of Christ in the Later Middle Ages." *Church History* 71 (2002): 685–714.

———. *Christian Materiality: An Essay on Religion in Late Medieval Europe.* Brooklyn: Zone Books, 2011.

———. *Wonderful Blood: Theology and Practice in Late Medieval Northern Germany and Beyond.* Philadelphia: University of Pennsylvania Press, 2007.

Cabrol, Fernand, and Henri Leclercq. *Dictionnaire d'archéologie chrétienne et de liturgie (DACL)*. 30 vols. Paris: Letouzey et Ané, 1907-1953.

Calvin, John. *Treatise on Relics, Translated from the French Original*. Translated by Count Valerian Krasinski. Edinburgh: Johnstone, Hunter, 1870. First published as *Traité des Reliques*, 1543.

Carruthers, Mary. *The Craft of Thought: Meditation, Rhetoric, and the Making of Images, 400-1200*. Cambridge: Cambridge University Press, 1998.

Cassidy-Welch, Megan, and Anne E. Lester, eds. *Crusades and Memory: Rethinking Past and Present*. London: Routledge, 2015.

Chaganti, Seeta. "Figure and Ground: *Elene*'s Nails, Cynewulf's Runes, and Hrabanus Maurus's Painted Poems." In Cooper and Denny-Brown, *Arma Christi*, 53-82.

Charlesworth, J. H. *The Odes of Solomon*. Oxford: Clarendon Press, 1973.

Chase, Christopher L. "'Christ III,' 'The Dream of the Rood,' and Early Christian Passion Piety." *Viator* 11 (1980): 11-33.

Chazelle, Celia. *The Crucified God in the Carolingian Era: Theology and Art of Christ's Passion*. Cambridge: Cambridge University Press, 2001.

Cohen, Meredith. *The Sainte-Chapelle and the Construction of Sacral Monarchy: Royal Architecture in Thirteenth-Century Paris*. New York: Cambridge University Press, 2015.

Conti, Roberto. "The Crown, the Treasury, and Theodelinda over Seven Centuries of Art in the Cathedral of Monza." In Buccellati, *Iron Crown*, 2:145-86.

Cooper, Lisa H., and Andrea Denny-Brown, eds. *The Arma Christi in Medieval and Early Modern Material Culture, with a Critical Edition of "O Vernicle."* Burlington, VT: Ashgate, 2014.

Cotsonis, John *Byzantine Figural Processional Crosses*. Dumbarton Oaks Byzantine Collection Publications 10. Washington, DC: Dumbarton Oaks Research Library and Collection, 1994.

Crosby, Sumner McKnight, William D. Wixom, Jane Hayward, and Charles T. Little. *The Royal Abbey of Saint-Denis in the Time of Suger (1122-1151)*. New York: Metropolitan Museum of Art, 1981.

Crossley, Paul. "The Politics of Presentation: the Architecture of Charles IV of Bohemia." In *Courts and Regions in Medieval Europe*, edited by Sarah Rees Jones, Richard Marks, and A. J. Minnis, 99-172. York: York Medieval Press, 2000.

de Blaauw, Sible. "Following the Crosses: The Processional Cross and the Typology of Processions in Medieval Rome." In *Christian Feast and Festival: The Dynamics of Western Liturgy and Culture*, edited by Paulus Gijsbertus and Johannes Post, 319–43. Liturgia Condenda 12. Leuven: Peeters, 2001.

Dennys, Rodney. *The Heraldic Imagination*. London: Barrie & Jenkins, 1975.

Douais, Célestin. "Deux reliquaires de l'église Saint Sernin à Toulouse." *Revue de l'art chrétien* 38 (1888): 154–69.

Drijvers, Jan Willem. *Helena Augusta: The Mother of Constantine the Great and the Legend of the Finding of the True Cross*. Leiden: Brill, 1992.

———. "Promoting Jerusalem: Cyril and the True Cross." In *Portraits of Spiritual Authority: Religious Power in Early Christianity, Byzantium, and the Christian Orient*, edited by Jan Willem Drijvers and John W. Watt, 79–95. Leiden: Brill, 1999.

Duffy, Eamon. *The Stripping of the Altars: Traditional Religion in England, 1400–1580*. New Haven, CT: Yale University Press, 1993.

Durand, Jannic, and Mathilde Avisseau-Broustet, eds. *Le trésor de la Sainte-Chapelle: Paris, Musée du Louvre, 31 mai–27 août 2001*. Paris: Réunion des musées nationaux, 2001.

Durliat, Marcel. "Théophanies-visions avec participation de prophètes dans la peinture romane catalane et toulousaine." *Comptes rendus des séances de l'Académie des Inscriptions et Belles-Lettres* 118 (1974): 536–64.

Edsall, Mary Agnes. "The *Arma Christi* before the *Arma Christi*: Rhetorics of the Passion in Late Antiquity and the Early Middle Ages." In Cooper and Denny-Brown, *Arma Christi*, 21–52.

Ehresmann, Donald. "The Iconography of the Cismar Altarpiece and the Role of Relics in an Early Winged Altarpiece." *Zeitschrift für Kunstgeschichte* 64 (2001): 1–36.

Elbern, Viktor H. "The Iron Crown of Monza: Appearance and Techniques." In Buccellati, *Iron Crown*, 2:199–204.

Engemann, Josef. "Zur Verbreitung magischer Übelabwehr in der nichtchristlichen und christlichen Spätantike." *Jahrbuch für Antike und Christentum* 18 (1985): 22–48.

Fajt, Jiří, ed. *Magister Theodoricus: Court Painter to Emperor Charles IV; The Pictorial Decoration of the Shrines at Karlštejn Castle*. Prague: National Gallery of Prague, 1998.

Fajt, Jiří, and Jan Royt. "The Pictorial Decoration of the Great Tower at Karlštejn Castle: Ecclesia Triumphans." In Fajt, *Magister Theodoricus*, 107-215.

Fernandez, Catherine. "Quidem lapis preciousus qui vocatur Cammaheu: The Medieval Afterlife of the Gemma Augustea." PhD diss., Emory University, 2012.

Fleming, John. "The Dream of the Rood and Anglo-Saxon Monasticism." *Traditio* 22 (1966): 43-72.

Folda, Jaroslav. *The Art of the Crusaders in the Holy Land, 1098-1187*. Cambridge: Cambridge University Press, 1995.

Foletti, Ivan. "The British Museum Casket with Scenes of the Passion: The Easter Liturgy and the Apse of St. John Lateran in Rome." In *The Fifth Century in Rome: Art, Liturgy, Patronage*, edited by Ivan Foletti and Manuela Gianandrea, 139-60. Rome: Viella, 2017.

Frank, Georgia. "Death in the Flesh: Picturing Death's Body and Abode in Late Antiquity." In *Looking Beyond: Visions, Dreams and Insights in Medieval Art and History*, edited by C. Hourihane, 58-74. State College: Penn State University Press, 2010.

Fricke, Beate. "A Liquid History: Blood and Animation in Late Medieval Art." *RES: Anthropology and Aesthetics* 63-64 (2013): 53-69.

Friede, Johannes. "Time and Eternity in the Eschatology of the Guennol Triptych." *Viator* 29 (1998): 363-76.

Frolow, Anton. *La relique de la Vraie Croix*. Paris: Institut Français d'Études Byzantines, 1961.

Gabrieli, Francesco. *Arab Historians of the Crusades*. Berkeley: University of California Press, 1969.

Gaborit-Chopin, Danielle, Elisabeth Taburet-Delahaye, Marie-Cécile Bardoz and Musée du Louvre. *Le trésor de Conques: Exposition du 2 novembre 2001 au 11 mars 2002, Musée du Louvre*. Paris: Editions du Patrimoine, 2001.

Gaposchkin, M. Cecilia. "From Pilgrimage to Crusade: The Liturgy of Departure, 1095-1300." *Speculum* 88 (2013): 44-91.

———. *Invisible Weapons: Liturgy and the Making of Crusade Ideology*. Ithaca, NY: Cornell University Press, 2017.

———. "The Place of Jerusalem in Western Crusading Rites of Departure." *Catholic Historical Review* 99 (2013): 1-29.

George, Philippe. "'Sur la terre comme au ciel': L'évêque de Liège, l'abbé de Stavelot-Malmedy, le droit, la justice et l'art mosan vers 1170." *Cahiers de civilisation médiévale* 56 (2013): 225–53.

Gussone, Nikolaus. "Adventus-Zeremoniell und Translation von Reliquien: Victricius von Rouen, De laude sanctorum." *Frühmittelalterliche Studien* 10 (1976): 125–33.

Hahn, Cynthia. "Collector and Saint: Queen Radegund and Devotion to the Relic of the True Cross." *Word and Image* 22 (2006): 268–74.

———. "Inscriptions and Interactions: Text and Image on the Cloisters Cross and Other Ivories." In *Inscriptions in Liturgical Spaces*, edited by Kristin B. Aavitsland and Turid Karlsen Seim, 185–204. Acta ad archaeologiam et artium historiam pertinentia, n.s. 10 (= vol. 24). Rome: Scienze e lettere, 2011.

———. "Portable Altars (and the Rationale): Liturgical Objects and Personal Devotion." In *Image and Altar 800–1300: Papers from an International Conference in Copenhagen, 24 October–27 October 2007*, edited by Poul Grinder-Hansen, 45–64. Publications from the National Museum Studies in Archaeology and History, Book 23. Copenhagen: University Press of Southern Denmark, 2014.

———. *Portrayed on the Heart: Narrative Effect in Pictorial Lives of Saints from the Tenth through the Thirteenth Century.* Berkeley: University of California Press, 2001.

———. *The Reliquary Effect: Enshrining the Sacred Object*, London: Reaktion Books, 2017.

———. "'The Sting of Death Is the Thorn, but the Circle of the Crown Is Victory over Death': The Making of the Crown of Thorns." In *Saints and Sacred Matter: The Cult of Relics in Byzantium and Beyond*, edited by Cynthia Hahn and Holger A. Klein, 193–214. Dumbarton Oaks Byzantine Symposia and Colloquia, Book 6. Washington, DC: Dumbarton Oaks Research Library and Collection, 2015.

———. *Strange Beauty: Issues in the Making and Meaning of Reliquaries, 400–circa 1204.* University Park: Penn State University Press, 2012.

Hamburger, Jeffrey F. "Frequentant memoriam visionis faciei meae." In *The Holy Face and the Paradox of Representation: Papers from a Colloquium Held at the Bibliotheca Hertziana, Rome and the Villa Spelman, Florence, 1996*, edited by H. L.

Kessler and G. Wolf, 229–46. Bologna: Nuova Alfa Editoriale, 1998. Distributed in the U.S. by Johns Hopkins University Press.

———. *Nuns as Artists: The Visual Culture of a Medieval Convent*. Berkeley: University of California Press, 1997.

———. *The Rothschild Canticles: Art and Mysticism in Flanders and the Rhineland circa 1300*. New Haven, CT: Yale University Press, 1990.

Heinlen, Michael. "An Early Image of a Mass of St. Gregory and Devotion to the Holy Blood at Weingarten Abbey." *Gesta* 37 (1998): 55–62.

Hennessy, Marlene. "The Disappearing Book in the Revelation of the Hundred Pater Nosters. Devotional Culture." In *Late Medieval England and Europe: Diverse Imaginations of Christ's Life*, edited by Stephen Kelly and Ryan Perry, 243–66. Turnhout, Belg.: Brepols, 2014.

———. "The Social Life of a Manuscript Metaphor: Christ's Blood as Ink." In *Manuscripts, Images, and Communities in the Late Middle Ages*, edited by Joyce Coleman, Mark Kruse, and Kathryn Smith, 17–52. Turnhout, Belg.: Brepols, 2013.

Hewitt, Joseph William. "The Use of Nails in the Crucifixion." *Harvard Theological Review* 25 (1932): 29–45.

Holloway, Julia. "The Dream of the Rood and Liturgical Drama." *Comparative Drama* 18 (1989): 119–37.

Holum, Kenneth. "Hadrian and St. Helena: Imperial Travel and the Origins of Christian Holy Land Pilgrimage." *The Blessings of Pilgrimage*, edited by Robert Ousterhout, 66–82. Urbana: University of Illinois Press, 1990.

Homolka, Jaromír. "The Pictorial Decoration of the Palace and Lesser Tower of Karlstejn Castle." In Fajt, *Magister Theodoricus*, 46–99.

Horrent, Jules. *Le Pèlerinage de Charlemagne: Essai d'explication littéraire avec des notes de critique textuelle*. Paris: Société d'Édition "Les Belles Lettres," 1961.

Jacobus de Voragine. *The Golden Legend: Readings on the Saints*. Princeton, NJ: Princeton University Press, 1993.

Jaspert, Nikolas. "The True Cross of Jerusalem in the Latin West: Mediterranean Connections and Institutional Agency." *Visual Constructs of Jerusalem*, edited by Bianca Kühnel, Galit Noga-Banai, and Hanna Vorholt, 207–22. Cultural Encounters in Late Antiquity and the Middle Ages, 18. Turnhout, Belg.: Brepols, 2014.

———. "Gedenkwesen und Erinnerung des Ordens vom Heiligen Grab." In *Wider das Vergessen und für das Seelenheil: Memoria und Totengedenken im Mittelalter,* edited by Rainer Berndt S. J., 149–74. Erudiri sapientia, 9. Münster: Aschendorff, 2013.

Jensen, Robin M. *The Cross: History, Art, and Controversy.* Cambridge, MA: Harvard University Press, 2017.

Kaegi, Walter. *Heraclius: Emperor of Byzantium.* Cambridge: Cambridge University Press, 2003.

Kirchweger, Franz, and Gunther G. Wolf. *Die Heilige Lanze in Wien: Insignie–Reliquie–"Schicksalsspeer."* Milan: Skira, 2005.

Kirkpatrick, Sidney. *Hitler's Holy Relics: A True Story of Nazi Plunder and the Race to Recover the Crown Jewels of the Holy Roman Empire.* New York: Simon & Schuster, 2010.

Klein, Holger. *Byzanz, der Westen, und das "wahre" Kreuz: Der Geschichte einer Reliquie und ihrer künstlerischen Fassung im Byzanz und im Abendland.* Wiesbaden: Reichert, 2004.

———. "Constantine, Helena, and the Early Cult of the True Cross in Constantinople." In *Byzance et les reliques du Christ,* edited by Jannic Durand and Bernard Flusin, 31–59. Paris: Centre de recherche d'histoire et civilisation de Byzance, 2004.

———. "Eastern Objects and Western Desires: Relics and Reliquaries between Byzantium and the West." *Dumbarton Oaks Papers* 58 (2004): 283–314.

Kühnel, Bianca. *From the Earthly to the Heavenly Jerusalem: Representations of the Holy City in Christian Art of the First Millennium.* Römische Quartalschrift für christliche Altertumskunde und Kirchengeschichte, Supplementheft 42. Rome: Herder, 1987.

Kumler, Aden. *Translating Truth: Ambitious Images and Religious Knowledge in Late Medieval France and England.* New Haven, CT: Yale University Press, 2011.

Ladner, Gerhart. "St. Gregory of Nyssa and St. Augustine on the Symbolism of the Cross." *Late Classical and Medieval Studies in Honor of Albert Mathias Friend Jr.,* edited by K. Weitzmann, 88–95. Princeton, NJ: Princeton University Press, 1955.

Lansdowne, John. "Broken but Not Divided: The Man of Sorrows in Byzantium." PhD diss., Princeton University, 2019.

Lewis, Flora. "Rewarding Devotion: Indulgences and the Promotion of Images." In *The Church and the Arts: Papers Read at the 1990 Summer Meeting and the 1991 Winter Meeting of the Ecclesiastical History Society*, edited by Diana Wood, 179-94. Oxford: Blackwell, 1995. Published for the Ecclesiastical History Society.

———. "The Wound in Christ's Side and the Instruments of Passion: Gendered Experience and Response." In *Women and the Book: Assessing the Visual Evidence*, edited by Jane H. M. Taylor and Lesley Smith, 204-29. London: British Library, 1996.

Lidov, Alexei. "A Byzantine Jerusalem: The Imperial Pharos Chapel as the Holy Sepulchre." In *Jerusalem as Narrative Space / Erzählraum Jerusalem*, edited by Annette Hoffmann and Gerhard Wolf, 63-103. Leiden: Brill, 2012.

Lyman, Thomas W. "Theophanic Iconography and the Easter Liturgy: The Romanesque Painted Program at Saint-Sernin de Toulouse." *Festschrift für Otto von Simson zum 65 Geburtstag*, edited by Lucius Grisebach and Konrad Renger, 72-93. Frankfurt a.M.: Propyläen Verlag, 1977.

MacCormack, Sabine. *Art and Ceremony in Late Antiquity*. Berkeley: University of California Press, 1981.

Mahler, Annemarie. "Lignum Domini and the Opening Vision of *The Dream of the Rood*: A Viable Hypothesis?" *Speculum* 53 (1978): 441-59.

Mély, Fernand de. *Exuviae sacrae constantinopolitanae*. Paris: Ernest Leroux, éditeur, 1904.

Merback, Mitchell B. "Fount of Mercy, City of Blood: Cultic Anti-Judaism and the Pulkau Passion Altarpiece." *Art Bulletin* 87 (2005): 589-642.

——— "The Man of Sorrows in Northern Europe: Ritual Metaphor and Therapeutic Exchange." *New Perspectives on the Man of Sorrows*, edited by Catherine Puglisi and William Barcham, 77-79. Kalamazoo, MI: Medieval Institute Publications, Western Michigan University, 2013.

———. *The Thief, the Cross and the Wheel: Pain and the Spectacle of Punishment in Medieval and Renaissance Europe*. Chicago: University of Chicago Press, 1998.

Mercuri, Chiara. *Corona di Christo, corona di re: La monarchia francese e la corona di spine nel medioevo*. Rome: Edizioni di storia e di letteratura, 2004.

Meurer, Heribert. "Andenken und Geschenke der Kreuzfahrer und Jerusalempilger in der Zeit der ersten Kreuzzüge." In *Transfer: Innovationen in der Zeit der*

*Kreuzzüge*, edited by Volker Herzner and Jürgen Krüger, 39–49. Speyer: Verlag der Pfälzischen Gesellschaft zur Förderung der Wissenschaften, 2006.

———. "Kreuzreliquiare aus Jerusalem." *Jahrbuch der Staatlichen Kunstsammlungen in Baden-Württemberg* 13 (1976): 7–18.

———. "Zu den Staurotheken der Kreuzfahrer." *Zeitschrift für Kunstgeschichte* 48 (1985): 65–76.

Mingana, A., ed. and trans. "Dadisho, Treatise on Solitude and Prayer," *Woodbroke Studies* 7 (1934): 70–143.

Migne, Jacques Paul. *Patrologiae cursus completus / Patrologia Graeca: . . . omnium ss. patrum, doctorum, scriptorumque ecclesiasticorum, . . ., sive Graecorum, qui ab aevo apostolico ad aetatem Innocenti III (ann. 1216).* Multivolume work. Paris, 1869 and other editions.

Migne, Jacques Paul. *Patrologiae cursus completus / Patrologia Latina: . . . omnium ss. patrum doctorum scriptorumque ecclesiasticorum, . . ., Series Latina.* Multivolume work. Paris, 1878 and other editions.

Murray, A. V. "'Mighty against the Enemies of Christ': The Relic of the True Cross in the Armies of the Kingdom of Jerusalem." *The Crusades and Their Sources: Essays Presented to Bernard Hamilton*, edited by John France and William G. Zajac, 217–38. Aldershot, UK: Ashgate, 1998.

Nagel, Alexander, and Christopher. S. Wood. *Anachronic Renaissance.* New York: Zone Books, 2010.

Ó Carragáin, Éamonn. *Ritual and the Rood: Liturgical Images and the Old English Poems of the Dream of the Rood Tradition.* London: British Library, 2005.

Opačić, Zoe. "Sacred Topography of Medieval Prague." In *Sacred Sites and Holy Places: Exploring the Sacralization of Landscape through Space and Time*, edited by S. W. Nordeide and S. Brink, 252–81. Turnhout, Belg.: Brepols, 2012.

Paris, Gaston. "La chanson du *Pèlerinage de Charlemagne*." *Romania: Revue trimestrielle consacrée à l'étude des langues et des littératures romanes* 9 (1880): 1–50.

Parshall, Peter, Rainer Schoch, et al. *Origins of European Printmaking: Fifteenth-Century Woodcuts and Their Public.* Exhibitions at National Gallery of Art, Washington, September 4–November 27, 2005; Germanisches Nationalmuseum, Nuremberg, December 14, 2005–March 19, 2006. New Haven, CT: Yale University Press, 2005.

Pastan, Elizabeth. "Charlemagne as Saint?: Relics and the Choice of Window Subjects at Chartres Cathedral." *The Legend of Charlemagne in the Middle Ages*, edited by Matthew Gabriele, 97–135. New York: Palgrave Macmillan US, 2008.

Pastan, Elizabeth, and Silvie Balcon. *Les vitraux du chœur de la cathédrale de Troyes (XIIIe siècle)*. Paris: Centre national de la recherche scientifique, 2006.

Paul, Nicholas, and Suzanne Yeager, eds. *Remembering the Crusades: Myth, Image, and Identity*. Rethinking Theory. Baltimore: Johns Hopkins University Press, 2012.

Peers, Glenn. *Sacred Shock: Framing Visual Experience in Byzantium*. University Park: Penn State University Press, 2004.

Piano, Natacha. "Passió de Crist: Espai litúrgic i política eclesiàstica a les pintures murals de Saint-Sernin de Toulouse." *Butlletí del Museu Nacional d'Art de Catalunya* 11 (2010): 117–25.

Pillepich, Alain. "Napoleon and the Iron Crown." In Buccellati, *Iron Crown*, 1:335–43.

Riley-Smith, Jonathan. *The First Crusade and the Idea of Crusading*. Philadelphia: University of Pennsylvania Press, 1986.

Rohault de Fleury, Charles. *Mémoire sur les instruments de la passion de N.-S.J.-C.* Paris: L. Lesort, 1870.

Rudy, Kathryn M. "Kissing Images, Unfurling Rolls, Measuring Wounds, Sewing Badges and Carrying Talismans: Considering Some Harley Manuscripts through the Physical Rituals they Reveal." *Electronic British Library Journal* (2011): 1–56.

Saalman, Howard, L. V. Ghirardini, and A. Law. "Recent Excavations under the 'Ombrellone' of Sant'Andrea in Mantua: Preliminary Report." *Journal of the Society of Architectural Historians* 51 (1992): 357–76.

Scarry, Elaine. *The Body in Pain: The Making and Unmaking of the World*. New York: Oxford University Press, 1985.

Shaw, Christine. "Peace-Making Rituals in Fifteenth-Century Siena." *Renaissance Studies* 20 (2006): 225–39.

Schier, V., and Corinne Schleif. "Seeing and Singing, Touching and Tasting the Holy Lance: The Power and Politics of Embodied Religious Experiences in Nuremberg 1424–1524." In *Signs of Change: Transformations of Christian*

Traditions and Their Representation in the Arts, 1000–2000, edited by C. Cluver, N. Bell, and N. H. Petersen, 401–26. Amsterdam: Rodopi, 2004.

Schiller, Gertrud. "The 'Arma Christi' and Man of Sorrows." In *Iconography of Christian Art*, 2:184–97. Translated by Janet Seligman. Greenwich, CT: New York Graphic Society, 1972.

Schulze-Dörrlamm, Mechthild. "Heilige Nägel und heilige Lanzen." In *Byzanz — das Römerreich im Mittelalter*, pt. 1, *Welt der Ideen, Welt der Dinge*, edited by Falko Daim and Jörg Drauschke, 1:97–171. Regensburg: Verlag des Römisch-Germanischen Zentralmuseums, 2010.

Scott, John Beldon. *Architecture for the Shroud: Relic and Ritual in Turin*. Chicago: University of Chicago Press, 2003.

Shagrir, Iris. "The Visitatio Sepulchri in the Latin Church of the Holy Sepulchre in Jerusalem." *Al-Masaq: Islam and the Medieval Mediterranean* 22 (2010): 57–77.

Spear, David S. "The School of Caen Revisited." *Haskins Society Journal: Studies in Medieval History* 4 (1992): 55–66.

Steinberg, Leo. *The Sexuality of Christ in Renaissance Art and in Modern Oblivion*. New York: Pantheon Books, 1983.

Suckale, Robert. "Arma Christi, Überlegungen zur Zeichenhaftigkeit mittelalterlicher Andachtsbilder." *Städel-Jahrbuch* Ser. NF, Bd. 6 (1977): 177–208.

Suckale, Robert, and Jiří Fajt. "The Circle of Charles IV." In Boehm and Fajt, *Prague: The Crown of Bohemia*, 35–45.

Szövérffy, Joseph. "'Crux Fidelis . . .' Prolegomena to a History of the Holy Cross Hymns." *Traditio* 22 (1966): 1–41.

Tammen, Silke. "Dorn und Schmerzensmann: Zum Verhältnis von Reliquie, Reliquiar und Bild in spätmittelalterlichen Christusreliquiaren." In *Reliquiare im Mittelalter*, edited by Bruno Reudenbach and Gia Toussaint, 189–208. Berlin: Akademie Verlag, 2005.

Theodulf, Bishop of Orléans. *Opus Caroli regis contra synodum (Libri Carolini)*. Monumenta Germaniae Historica, Leges, Concilia, T. 2, Suppl. 1. Hannover: Hahnsche Buchhandlung, 1998.

Thomas à Kempis. *Meditations on the Life of Christ*. Translated by Samuel Kettlewell and H. P. Wright. Oxford, 1892.

Thuno, Erik. *Image and Relic: Mediating the Sacred in Early Medieval Rome*. Rome: "L'Erma" di Bretschneider, 2002.

Treharne, Elaine, trans. "The Dream of the Rood." In *Old and Middle English Anthology*. Edited by Elaine Treharne. Oxford: Blackwell, 2000.
Underhill, Evelyn. "The Fountain of Life: An Iconographical Study." *Burlington Magazine* 17, no. 86 (1910): 99–101.
Van Tongeren, Louis. *Exaltation of the Cross: Toward the Origins of the Feast of the Cross and the Meaning of the Cross in Early Medieval Liturgy*. Leuven: Peeters, 2000.
Verdier, Philippe. "Les staurothèques mosanes et leurs iconographie du Jugement Dernier." *Cahiers de civilisation médiévale, Xe-XIIe siècles* 16 (1973): 97–121, 199–213.
Vincent, Nicholas. *The Holy Blood: King Henry III and the Westminster Blood Relic*. Cambridge: Cambridge University Press, 2001.
Wall, J. Charles. *The Relics of the Passion*. London: Talbot, 1910.
Walsh, P. G., trans. and annot. *Letters of St. Paulinus of Nola*. Westminster, MD: Newmann Press, 1967.
Watin-Grandchamp, D., P. Cabau, et al. "Le coffret reliquaire de la Vraie Croix de Saint-Sernin de Toulouse." *Les cahiers de Saint-Michel de Cuxa* 38 (2007): 37–46.
Westermann-Angerhausen, Hiltrud. "Das Nagelreliquiar im Trierer Egbertschrein: Das 'künstlerisch edelste Werk der Egbertwerkstätte'?" *Festschrift für Peter Bloch*, edited by Hartmut Krohm and Christian Theuerkauff, 9–23. Mainz: P. von Zabern, 1990.
Wharton, Annabel Jane. *Selling Jerusalem: Relics, Replicas, Theme Parks*. Chicago: University of Chicago Press, 2006.
Whitman, Jon. "Transfers of Empire, Movements of Mind: Holy Sepulcher and Holy Grail." *Modern Language Notes* 123 (2008): 895–923.
Wilmowsky, Johann Nikolaus. *Der Dom zu Trier in seinen drei Hauptperioden: Der römischen, der fränkischen, der romanischen, beschrieben und durch XXVI Tafeln erläutert*. Trier, 1874.
Willems, Christoph. *Der hl. Rock zu Trier: Eine archäologisch-historische Untersuchung*. Trier, 1891.
Woolf, Rosemary. "The Theme of Christ the Lover-Knight in Medieval English Literature." *Review of English Studies* 13, no. 49 (1962): 1–16.
Wortley, John. "The Legend of Constantine the Relic-Provider." In *Studies on the Cult of Relics in Byzantium up to 1204*, 487–96. Burlington, VT: Ashgate/Variorum, 2009.

ILLUSTRATIONS

1. Titian (Tiziano Vecelli), *The Vendramin Family*, National Gallery, London   2
2. *Stavelot Triptych*, Morgan Library and Museum, New York   9
3. *Stavelot Triptych* (detail), Morgan Library and Museum, New York   10
4. *Apse Mosaic of the Ark of the Covenant*, Oratory of Germigny-des-Prés, France   12
5. *"Quadriga of Aminadab"* (detail from Allegories of Saint Paul window), Abbey Church, Saint-Denis, France   14
6. *Triptych Reliquary of the Cross*, Wyvern Collection, United Kingdom   16
7. "Scenes of the Life of the Martyr Romanus," in Prudentius, *Carmina*, Burgerbibliothek, Bern   18
8. *The Death of Judas and the Crucifixion*, British Museum, London   19
9. *Pilate and Christ Carrying the Cross*, British Museum, London   20
10. Gentile Bellini, *Procession of the True Cross*, Gallerie dell'Accademia, Venice   22–23
11. *Pectoral Reliquary Cross* (front and back), British Museum, London   25
12. *Scheldewindeke Cross*, Church of St. Christopher, Scheldewindeke, Belgium   28

13. "Public Showing of the True Cross Relic by Louis IX," in Matthew Paris, *Chronica Maiora II*, Parker Library, Cambridge   *33*
14. *Jerusalem Cross from Denkendorf*, Städtische Kunstsammlungen, Augsburg   *36*
15. *Limoges Reliquary Cross*, Metropolitan Museum of Art, New York   *37*
16. "Helena Discovering the True Cross," *Reliquary of the True Cross* (side view), Basilique Saint-Sernin, Musée Saint-Raymond, Toulouse   *39*
17. "Marys at the Tomb and Scenes of the Donation of a Cross," *Reliquary of the True Cross*, Basilique Saint-Sernin   *40*
18. "Majestas (Rev 12:15–19) and Further Scenes of the Donation of a Cross," *Reliquary of the True Cross*, Basilique Saint-Sernin   *41*
19. Holy Nails, in Charles Rohault de Fleury, *Mémoire sur les instruments de la passion de N.-S. J.-C.*, Ingalls Library, Cleveland Museum of Art   *54*
20. *Icon with the Crucifixion*, Metropolitan Museum of Art, New York   *57*
21. *Five Good Emperors* (detail of trophies of Dacian weapons), National Historical Museum, Bucharest   *59*
22. *Passion Sarcophagus* (detail), Vatican Museums, Vatican City   *60*
23. Detail of illustration for Psalm 21/22, *Utrecht Psalter*, Utrecht University Library   *61*
24. *Tympanum of Sainte-Foi* (detail), Church of Sainte-Foi, Conques   *62*
25. *Reliquary of the Holy Nail*, Cathedral Treasury, Trier   *67*
26. *Titulus Crucis*, Santa Croce in Gerusalemme, Rome   *69*
27. *The Melismos*, Church of St. John the Baptist, Axos, Mylopotamos, Crete   *70*
28. *The Holy Lance*, Kunsthistorisches Museum, Vienna   *72*
29. "Invention of the Holy Lance in Jerusalem," in Sébastien Mamerot, *Passages d'outremer*, Bibliothèque nationale de France, Paris   *74*
30. *Holy Robe in Trier*, Trier Cathedral, Trier   *75*
31. "Translation of the Holy Blood," in Matthew Paris, *Chronica Maiora II*, Parker Library, Cambridge   *77*
32. *Reliquary of the Blood of Christ* ("Beirut ampulla"), Santa Maria Della Scala, Siena   *78*

33. *Charlemagne Offers Relics to Chartres*, Chartres Cathedral, France   83
34. Shaun Leane for Alexander McQueen, *"Crown of Thorns" Headpiece and "Thorn" Armpiece*, Metropolitan Museum, New York   84
35. *Archbishop Gauthier Cornut of Sens Displaying the Crown of Thorns*, Metropolitan Museum of Art, New York   86
36. Sainte-Chapelle (interior), Paris   87
37. *Reliquary of the Thorn*, Abbey of Saint-Maurice d'Agaune, Switzerland   89
38. *Coronation Cross of Bohemia*, Treasury of the St. Vitus Cathedral, Prague   93
39. Nicholas Wurmser of Strasbourg, *Charles Receiving Relics of the Passion and Placing Them in the Cross*, Karlštejn Castle, Czech Republic   94
40. Master Theodoric and Workshop, Chapel of The Holy Cross, Karlštejn Castle, Czech Republic   95
41. Guarino Guarini (architect), Chapel of the Holy Shroud (interior), Turin Cathedral   97
42. Antonio Tempesta, *The Annual Display of the Holy Shroud in Turin on 4 May*, British Museum, London   100
43. Carlo Dolci, *St. Catherine of Siena*, Dulwich Picture Gallery, London   102
44. *Vine of Christ*, Diocesan and Cathedral Museum, Valladolid   104
45. "Arma Christi," in Kolda of Koldice, *Passionale of Abbess Kunigunde*, National Library of the Czech Republic, Prague   106
46. Bohemian artist, *Reliquary with the Man of Sorrows*, Walters Art Museum, Baltimore, Maryland   108
47. "The Veronica," in Matthew Paris, *Chronica Maiora II*, Parker Library, Cambridge   110
48. Detail of illustration for Psalm 114/115, *Utrecht Psalter*, Utrecht University Library   113
49. "Kunigunde before Christ, the Lance," in Kolda of Koldice, *Passionale of Abbess Kunigunde*, National Library of the Czech Republic, Prague   115
50. "Sponsa and Man of Sorrows," Beinecke Rare Book and Manuscript Library, Yale University, New Haven, Connecticut   116–17

INDEX

Adhemar, bishop of Le Puy, 45, 46
adventus ceremony, 42, 77, 80
Aelred of Rievaulx, saint, *De institutis inclusarum*, 103
Agaune, Monastery of Saint-Maurice, 88, *fig.* 37
Agritius, saint, Bishop of Trier, 73
Albigensian Crusade, 43
Alcuin, 27
Ambrose, saint, bishop of Milan, 66, 68
Andrew, Apostle, 46
angels, 15, 27, 43, 44, 60, 63, 75, 76, 94, 100, 112, 125n56
Anselm, saint, 103
Antioch, siege of, 45, 73
Ark of the Covenant, 11, 13, 15, *fig.* 4, 5
Arma Christi, 6, 34, 53, 60, 67, 90, 103-111, 112, 122n10
Arnulf of Chocques, 46-47, 49
Augustine, saint, bishop of Hippo, 28-29
audience, 3, 5, 43, 48-49, 68, 105

Baldwin II, Latin emperor of Constantinople, 84-85
Bellini, Gentile, 21, *fig.* 10
Bern, Burgerbibliothek, Cod. 264, Prudentius, *Carmina*, 17, *fig.* 7
Bernard of Clairvaux, saint, 103
Blanche of Castile, 84
blood, 3, 4, 11, 13, 25-27, 30, 55-56, 63, 70, 85, 90, 98, 103, 107, 111, 114, 129n57; Beirut ampullae, 79, 131n78, *fig.* 32; Blood (Holy), relics, 76-79, *fig.* 31
body, bodies, 3, 21-22, 29, 52-53, 58, 112, 123-4n30; broken, 55; Christ's body, 4, 21, 27, 29, 51-53, 55-56, 58, 67, 98-100, 103, 105, 118
Bonaventure, saint, 88, 103; *Lignum vitae* and *Vitis mystica*, 103
Bruges, Basilica of the Holy Blood, 79

Calvin, John, *Treatise on Relics*, 7
*Chanson de Roland*, 68

Charlemagne, emperor, 31, 42, 67, 68, 82, 91, 94, *fig.* 33
Charles IV, Holy Roman Emperor, 76, 91–96, 101, 107, *fig.* 40
Charles the Bald, emperor, 31, 66–67
Chartres, Cathedral of Notre Dame, 82, *fig.* 33
chi-rho, 8, 58
column of flagellation, relic, 76, 80, 107, 114
community, 1, 3, 49, 80
Conques, Ste-Foi, 35, 63, *fig.* 24
Constantine, emperor, 7–8, 17–18, 30, 58, 59, 66
Constantinople, 8, 30–31, 34, 42, 66, 70, 75–76, 80–82, 84, 111; column, 30, 124n34; Hagia Sophia 75, 80; Pharos, Palace chapel, 80; sack of 1204, 32, 76, 80–1
Cornut, Gauthier, bishop of Sens, 85, *fig.* 35
cross, 1, 8, 17, 51, 58, 63, 65, 68, 100, 103, 109, 114; animated, 26–27, 52, 112, 123n24; body and, 21, 24, 27–29, 32, 67; changeability and multivalence, 19–21, 25–26, 49–50, 107; gemmed, 8, 25, 26–28, 35, 92; liturgical, 19, 31, 43–44, 45; Liturgy of Exaltation of, 24–25; living/green, 13, 26–27, 30, 52; Orthodox or Patriarchal Cross, 32–34, 38, *fig.* 13; material of, 6, 8, 11, 13, 15, 17, 18, 21, 24, 27–28, 32, 48, 50, 52–53, 64, 81; pectoral, 24, *fig.* 11; prayer to, 24, 26–28, 30, 40, 50, 123n30; as sign, 8, 11, 13, 15, 17–19, 29, 31–2, 44, 48, 60, 122n13; theatricality of, 11, 29, 49–50. *See also* Cross (True), relic
Cross (True), relic, 1, 6–11, 13, 15, 18, 21, 24–25, 29, 30–34, 38–50, 52–53, 64–65, 68, 75–77, 80–85, 90, 91, 95–96, 98, 105, 107, 111, 126n4; dissemination, 7, 8–9, 29, 31–34; imperial sign and standard, 8, 17–18, 59, 111; Jerusalem (Crusader) cross, 34–50, *fig.* 14; reliquary, 1, 15, 21, 24, 26, 29, 34, 38–50, 91–92, 111, *fig.* 1, 2, 6, 10, 12, 14–18, 38–39, 46; splinter, 1, 7–8, 29–30, 82, 95, 98
Crown of Thorns/thorn (Holy), relic, 5, 15, 32, 53–55, 58, 63, 64, 75–77, 80, 82–90, 92, 95, 96–98, 101–102, 107, 112, 118, *fig.* 34, 35, 37
Crucifixion, 1, 4, 8, 19, 27, 52, 58, 63–4, 70, 76–7, 94, 122n12, *fig.* 8, 20
Crusades, crusader, 6, 30–8, 44–50, 52, 63–64, 73, 79–82, 85, 98.
Crusader cross. *See* Cross (True), relic, Jerusalem (Crusader) cross
crystal, rock, 1, 15, 27, 88, 91, *fig.* 6, 12, 37, 38
Cynewulf *Elene*, 65
Cyril, bishop of Jerusalem, 7–8, 29, 30

devotion, 2–6, 24–29, 47, 49, 52–3, 56, 65, 67, 71, 76, 77, 79, 90, 91–92, 98–100, 101–118
*Dream of the Rood*, 26–27, 50, 112

Eckebert of Schönau, *Stimulus amoris*, 65, 114
Eusebius, bishop of Caesarea, 17, 122n4

foreskin of Christ, relic, 121n2, 127n14
Francis, Saint, 24

Garnier de Traînel, bishop of Troyes, 81
Geoffrey de Charny, 98
Germigny-des-Prés, 11, 15, *fig.* 4
Gerold, Abbot of Saint-Maurice in Senlis, 88
Gertrude of Helfta, *Legatus divinae pietatis*, 107–109

Grace/reconciliation/redemption, 11–13, 48, 79
Grail (Holy), 76–77
Gregory of Tours, saint, bishop, 75
Guarini, Guarino, 96–98, *fig.* 41

Helena, empress, 7–8, 18, 30, 38, 64–66, 68, 73, 122n3, *fig.* 2, 3
Henry III, King of England, 77
Heraclius, Byzantine emperor, 8, 31, 75, 80
Honorius III, pope, 35

*Imago Pietatis. See* Man of Sorrows
indulgences, 92, 98, 105–7, 118
Innocent III, pope, 105
Innocent IV, pope, 107
Innocent VIII, pope, 70

Jacobus de Voragine, 109
Jerusalem, 6–8, 24–25, 30–32, 35–50, 70, 75–76, 77, 80, 82, 92, 98, 118; Church of Sion, 70, 80; Heavenly Jerusalem, 47–48, 92; Holy Sepulcher, 35, 43, 47–48, 70, 80, 90, 96; Monastery of our Lady Josaphat, 38, 47; Order of the Sepulcher, 48
John of Fécamp, 103

Karlštejn, Palace, 91–96, 101, *fig.* 39, 40
Kolda of Koldice, *Passionale of Abbess Kunigunde*, 114, *fig.* 45, 49

Lance (Holy), relic, 6, 45–47, 58–59, 63, 64, 66, 68–73, 75, 80, 90, 98, 111–119, *fig.* 27, 28, 29, 49, 50
Last Judgment, 15, 60–62, 112
London, British Museum, Ivory Plaques, 19–20, *fig.* 8, 9
Louis, Duke of Savoy, 98
Louis IX, Saint, King of France, 32, 34, 43, 70, 76–77, 84–90, 91, 98, 101

Mamerot, Sébastien, *Passages d'outremer*, 73, *fig.* 29
*Mandylion*, relic, 90
Man of Sorrows/*Imago Pietatis*, 105, 107, *fig.* 46, 50
Mass of St. Gregory, 107
Materiality/ material, 2–6, 8, 11, 13, 21, 32, 46, 50, 51–53, 56, 63–66, 71, 76, 81, 88, 98–99, 111, 119. *See also* relics, materiality; cross, material of
Matthew Paris, Monk of St Albans, 32, 77, *fig.* 13, 31, 47
*Meditations on the Life of Christ*, 103
Melisende, Queen, 47

Nails (Holy), relic, 6, 52, 53–54, 58, 63–68, 71, 73, 80, 82, 97, 112, 114, 118, 127n19, 128n33, *fig.* 19, 24, 25
Napoleon Bonaparte, 66

*O Vernicle*, 109

Paris: Sainte-Chapelle, 32, 70, 73, 85, 88, 90, 91, 96, 105, 111, 127n14, *fig.* 36; Cathedral of Notre Dame, 53, 101
Passion, narration, 19–20, 29, 38–40, 51, 55, 98–100, 103, 119
Passion Relics: and absence, 4; collected/ collections, as a group, ix, 52–53, 55, 63, 76, 79–82, 90–92, 96–98, 101, 109; definition 1, 3–5; devotional use, 6, 34, 51, 52, 76, 90, 99–119; Dominical relics, 4; instruments of torture/ weapons, 4, 20, 51, 55–56, 58, 60, 68, 75, 104–5, 111–112, 114; imperial use, 5–6, 60, 71, 92, 101., 15, 60–63, *fig.* 6, 24; life-saving, 15; political use, 53, 56, 77, 79–82, 96, 101, 111; provenance, 5, 30, 34, 38, 64, 68; represented in art, 21, 63–64; trophies of victory, 6, 58–60, 104. See also

Passion Relics *(continued)*
   *Arma Christi;* Blood (Holy), relic; column of flagellation, relic; Crown of Thorns/Thorn (Holy), relic; Cross (True), relic; Cross (True), relic, imperial sign and standard; Last Judgment imagery; *Mandylion*, relic; Nail (Holy), relic; Lance (Holy), relic; relic/s; reliquary; Robe (Holy); Sponge (Holy), relic; Stone of Unction, relic; Titulus (Title board of Cross), relic; Turin Shroud (Holy), relic; Veronica, relic
Paulinus, bishop of Nola, 30
*Le Pèlerinage de Charlemagne,* 82
Peter Bartholomew, monk, 46–47
Philip de Mezières, 32
pilgrimage/pilgrims, 6, 8, 24, 31, 35, 40, 42, 48, 73, 76, 80, 130n63
Prague, 76, 91, 95; Cathedral of Saint Vitus, 91
procession, 20, 21–24, 35, 47, 79, 81, *fig.* 10
Prudentius. *See* Bern, Burgerbibliothek

Quadriga of Aminadab, 13, *fig.* 5
*Quem Quaeritis,* 43–44

Radegund, Saint, Queen of Franks, 31, 38
Raymond Botardelli, 38–43
Raymond IV, Count of Toulouse, 42, 45, 46
relic/s: authenticity/truth, 4, 64, 79; contingency, 4, 5; definition, 3, 5, 24–25, 30; gift, 7, 8, 31–32, 35, 38, 42–43, 73, 79, 81, 85, 87–88, 91–92, 107; light-emitting, 27, 52, 65, 88, 99; materiality, 2–3, 11, 13, 7, 52, 65, 71, 119; means of Selection, 3; memory, 3; Old Testament, 15; redirection, 3.
*See also* Passion relics, reliquary; cross, material of; materiality/materials
reliquary: importance for framing and visibility, 1–4, 90; rhetoric of staging, 4, 11. *See also* Cross (True), relic; reliquary
resurrection, 4, 8, 43, 47, 49, 55, 109, 125
Rita of Cascia, saint, 102
Robe (Holy), relic, 58, 73, *fig.* 30
Rohault de Fleury, Charles, 53–4, *fig.* 19
Romanos, hymnist, 58
Romanus, saint, 17, *fig.* 7
Rome, 8, 24, 30, 73; Lateran Basilica, and Sancta Sanctorum, 76, 96; Santa Croce in Gerusalemme, 66, 68, 76, 107, *fig.* 26; St. Peter's Basilica, 70

Saint-Denis, Abbey Church, 13, 67, 130n63, *fig.* 5
senses, 3, 25, 76, 100, 109, 114, 118. *See also* vision/visions/visibility
Sophronius of Jerusalem, 75
Sponge (Holy), relic, 59, 73–6, 80, 90, 92, 95, 119
Stavelot Triptych (Morgan Library and Museum), 34, *fig.* 2, 3
*Stimulus amoris. See* Eckebert of Schönau
Stone of Unction, relic, 80, 90
Suger, abbot of Saint-Denis, 13

Tabernacle and Temple, 11, 13, 44, 65
Tempesta, Antonio, 99, *fig.* 42
Theoderic, Master, 92, *fig.* 40
Thierry, Count of Flanders, 79
Thiofrid of Echternach, 65–66, 71, 131n82
Thomas à Kempis, *Prayers and Meditations on the Life of Christ,* 90, 130n69
Thorn (Holy), relic. *See* Crown of Thorns
throne of mercy, 11–12

Titian (Tiziano Vecelli), 1–3, *fig.* 1
Titulus (Title board of Cross), relic, 27, 34, 64, 68, *fig.* 26
Toulouse, Saint-Sernin, 38–50, 81; Limoges cross reliquary, 38–50, 112, *fig.* 16–18; Pons, Abbot, 40, 125n56
*translatio imperii*, 101, 118
Troyes, Cathedral of Saint-Pierre-et-Saint-Paul, 81, 98
Turin Cathedral and Chapel of Holy Shroud, 96–98, *fig.* 41
Turin Shroud (Holy), relic, 73, 96–101, 119, 130n65, *fig.* 42

Utrecht Psalter, 58, 112, 132n97, *fig.* 23, 48

Venantius Fortunatus, bishop, 31
Vendramin Family, 1, *fig.* 1
Venice, Scuola Grande di San Giovanni Evangelista, 1, 21, 32, *fig.* 1, 10
Veronica, relic, 73, 105, 107–9, *fig.* 49
virtues, 15, 28, 112, 131n82
vision/visions/visibility, 1–2, 8, 13, 17, 21, 24–27, 44, 46, 48, 88, 90, 92, 95, 99, 107, 109, 111
*Visitatio Sepulchri*, 43–45

wounds of Christ, 15, 70–71, 94–95, 100, 105, 111, 114, 118
Wyvern Collection, *Triptych Reliquary of the True Cross*, 15, 75, 105, *fig.* 6

## BIBLICAL CITATIONS

| | | | |
|---|---|---|---|
| Exod. 25:17 | 11 | Matt. 24:30 | 15, 60 |
| Exod. 26:20 | 15 | Matt. 27:48 | 73 |
| Lev. 2:5–6 | 55 | Mark 15:36 | 73 |
| 1 Chron. 29:2 | 65 | John 19:19–20 | 68 |
| Josh. 6:19 | 65 | John 19:23–24, | 73 |
| Isa. 53:7, 10 | 55 | John 19:29 | 75 |
| Ezek. 1:1–26 | 13 | 1 Cor 1:17–18 | 17 |
| Zech 12:10 | 122n9 | 1 Cor. 11:24 | 55 |
| Zech 14:20 | 66 | Heb. 9:4 | 13 |
| Ps. 21:19, 29, 32 | 58–60 | Heb. 9:11–12 | 13 |
| Ps. 131:14 | 118 | Rev. 12:15–19 | 44, *fig.* 18 |

Founded in 1893,
UNIVERSITY OF CALIFORNIA PRESS
publishes bold, progressive books and journals
on topics in the arts, humanities, social sciences,
and natural sciences—with a focus on social
justice issues—that inspire thought and action
among readers worldwide.

The UC PRESS FOUNDATION
raises funds to uphold the press's vital role
as an independent, nonprofit publisher, and
receives philanthropic support from a wide
range of individuals and institutions—and from
committed readers like you. To learn more, visit
ucpress.edu/supportus.